Robin's Song

Robert D. Petrik
Robin D. Petrik (decd)

TRILOGY CHRISTIAN PUBLISHERS
TUSTIN, CA

Trilogy Christian Publishers
A Wholly Owned Subsidiary of Trinity Broadcasting Network
2442 Michelle Drive
Tustin, CA 92780

Robin's Song

Trilogy Christian Publishers A Wholly Owned Subsidiary of Trinity Broadcasting Network

2442 Michelle Drive Tustin, CA 92780

Cover design by: Jeff Summers

For information about special discounts for bulk purchases, please contact Trilogy Christian Publishing.

Manufactured in the United States of America

10 9 8 7 6 5 4 3 2 1

Library of Congress Cataloging-in-Publication Data is available.

ISBN: 978-1-68556-163-5

E-ISBN: 978-1-68556-164-2

Dedication

My loving wife and partner of fifty-six years (decd),

Kay Petrik,

mother, nurse, nutritionist, caretaker.

ROBIN DYAN PETRIK

December 24, 1969-December 30, 1983

Contents

Introduction

Have you ever wondered why life seems so complicated? Almost every day, problems come up! Each of us experiences these without fail. For this reason, I would like to share some of myself and my family with you. Robin was a pioneer in the development of early childhood chronic peritoneal dialysis and was the youngest successful recipient of a kidney transplant. Since that time, countless children have lived because of what she went through.

I want you to discover with me how God worked out His plan for Robin's life. She was an ordinary young lady whom God made special. Maybe this can help us in understanding ourselves better by understanding how our family and Robin used God's Word to work through difficulties and questions. Many of these are the same questions and similar-type circumstances you may or may have encountered.

At birth, each of us starts a journey. I prefer to think of this as an adventure. We never really know from one day to the next if excitement or disaster awaits. Moreover, it is difficult to predict when our lives will be complete. At first, our parent or parents help us along, but eventually, we must go it alone. Success or failure will be measured by the choices we make daily.

Robin's adventure is complete. Robin's Song is to honor God and, by letting you understand her life, to help make your life more meaningful.

1

The Unexpected

Kay and I met while attending college. I was taking an extra quarter to finish my degree. Kay was a senior. We discovered each other through a blind date! Shortly afterward, we started getting seriously involved and, by Christmas, were engaged. I completed my degree, then graduated, and was commissioned as an officer with the Corps of Engineers in February. My orders directed me to report to Fort Belvoir, Virginia, for additional training. I would be there for eleven weeks.

We set our wedding in May when I completed schooling. Kay would stay out spring term and finish her degree program during summer school.

Our plans worked perfectly. I received orders for duty in Germany. There was a waiting list for dependent travel, which meant Kay would not be able to join me until fall. We were stationed there for more than three years. Coming out of university, getting married, and going overseas was an exciting experience. What a fun way to start married life!

After Europe, I spent a year in Vietnam before leaving active duty. I served as a company commander, captain. Kay spent the year living and working near her family. She was an only child; they appreciated having her nearby. Also, it was nice for her to make the adjustments to being back in the States in familiar surroundings. She was hired by an insurance company and worked as an inside-claims representative.

My first civilian job was in Portland, Oregon. I was a trust representative (for farm and ranch) with one of the banks. Shortly after, Kay's company transferred her to Portland. We both enjoyed living in the area. However, I did not adjust well to being inside and behind a desk! I decided outside sales would be better and became an insurance agent.

A few months later, I was offered an agency manager's position with a farm-oriented insurance company. We would be moving to Pendleton, Oregon. Kay and I were excited about moving. Kay was thrilled with the idea of becoming a full-time housewife and mother. Both of us were anxious to start our family. It was an easy decision to make.

Christmas has always been our favorite time of year. We delight in celebrating the birth of our Savior. Also, we had fond memories of holidays spent in Germany, especially Christmas. This year, 1969, we planned a nice quiet first Christmas in Pendleton. Kay was expecting our first child in mid-January. Being late in her pregnancy, she did not want many extra activities.

We received a special Christmas Eve surprise! Slightly ahead of schedule, our baby daughter arrived on the twenty-fourth. The nurses even presented her to us in a big red Christmas stocking. We were indeed pleased and overjoyed.

The next few days went very quickly. We celebrated Christmas at the hospital while making plans for our baby's homecoming. Kay and I had spent time unsuccessfully trying to decide on a name. Finally, we worked out a solution. She would choose the names; however, they would all have the same R D initials as their dad's. The new mother picked Robin Dyan. A lovely name for a beautiful daughter!

Robin
Strength of Character

"Whatever you do, work at it with all your heart, as working for the Lord, not for men" (Colossians 3:23).

According to an old English legend, the robin mercifully removed a thorn from Christ's crown as He was on the way to Calvary. As the bird flew away, a drop of His blood fell on its breast, dyeing it red. We found this especially interesting since the importance of Christ's birth was the subsequent shedding of His blood on the cross.

Kay chose Dyan for Robin's middle name. The unique spelling was borrowed from the first name of Kay's favorite movie actress, Dyan Cannon.

The day to bring Robin home arrived. Suddenly, our joy was overcome by uncertainty. Her doctor came into the room and said, "We've discovered your daughter was born with an imperforate anus (malformed rectum). There may be other birth defects as well. I have arranged for you to take her directly to Portland for tests."

As the reality began to set in, our hearts were flooded with disbelief and concern. Why had they not told us sooner? What did it mean? How serious was this? Our doctor did not have answers and politely suggested to us that a specialist was waiting for our arrival in Portland.

Quite honestly, because of the holiday time of year, the doctor had not noticed any problems. Most babies are born normal, so there had not seemed to be any need for special concern. One of the nurses had made the discovery.

We made record time driving the two hundred miles to Portland. It seemed odd not taking our new baby home. The trip was an uneasy one as we kept asking each other what to expect. When we arrived in Portland, a doctor was literally waiting for us in the lobby of the hospital.

They immediately began a series of tests and an evaluation. To complete this took the better part of a week. Most of the time, we knew little about what was going on. However, Robin seemed to be doing all right. The doctors found in addition to the imperforate (not formed) anus, her lower backbone was slightly underdeveloped. They were unable to determine any other irregularities. These conditions are classified as congenital, birth defects.

The results of the tests and examination revealed a small opening leading to the vagina. Solids possibly could be eliminated through this until corrective surgery was completed. The lower spine, the doctor felt, would never be a problem. This occasionally happens with an early birth.

Finally, we were able to take our precious Robin home! First, new babies are fun. Feeding them and watching them respond and change is fascinating. Kay and I enjoyed making the adjustment to our new role as parents. We were especially thankful the problems were not more serious. Doctors assured us that, with time and medical help (minor surgery when she was older), she would develop and grow into a healthy child.

The next couple of months did not go as well as we had hoped. Constipation was a continual problem. Consequently, during the first year, she had two surgeries to correct the defect. During the second operation, she was given a colostomy. This would be used while the area healed so the doctors could be sure it was correct this time. All these experiences were totally new to Kay and me, but our faith remained strong. We felt, in the end, the problem would be solved and we would be back to normal.

We accepted the situation feeling God was in charge. While we do not always understand why things happen, we felt, with His help, we would get through. Keeping busy and constantly on the go did not leave much time to dwell on the negative aspect of birth defects. Robin was an incredibly good baby, a real charmer. She did not seem to mind the changing scenery of the trips we took. This eased the burden.

At Easter time, Robin was three months old; we drove over to Eastern Montana. My parents were retiring. They had sold their ranch and were closing things out with an auction sale. This also gave us an excuse to show off our new little one.

Two weeks after returning, we went to the Pacific coast for a company meeting. Then a brief time later, I had another meeting in Reno, Nevada. This time, however, Robin stayed with her grandma and grandpa, the Nelsons, in Springfield, Oregon.

My agency was doing well. So well, in fact, Kay and I were rewarded with a cruise to Jamaica. Unfortunately, Robin could not go. She again stayed with her grandparents. We enjoyed our vacation aboard the cruise ship Starward. Shipboard life was relaxing with three ports of call, including one at Kingston, very enjoyable. One of the more memorable fun things we did was to raft down on one of the rivers on a banana boat. Kay did miss her baby, and the minute we arrived back in Miami, she was on the phone, checking in. Grandma and Robin were doing fine.

Robin's first birthday and Christmas were great. Both sets of grandparents came to visit the new granddaughter. She was walking and had her first teeth; three came in all at one time. Much to my delight, her first words were "Da Da"! With two sets of grandparents bringing presents plus the new parents not wanting to be outdone, she had plenty of gifts to open. Robin enjoyed everything, the attention more than the gifts. Kay and I had a real sense of peace about her medical difficulties. We were thankful for God's provision and had confidence these would be overcome.

Our plans for the new year were taking shape. Kay was expecting our second child in June, and we were anticipating another move. I had always wanted to ranch, having grown up with that lifestyle. After moving to Pendleton, we had been looking for a wheat ranch to buy. We had finally found just the right place. In the next few months, we would have to sell our house in town, finish up the details for purchasing the ranch, and move while getting ready for our new addition. I planned to continue working for the business in town, doing ranch work with hired help. We decided this would be best until we were ready to become full-time ranchers.

In February, the doctor in Portland closed off the colostomy. Kay and Robin went from the hospital to their grandma and grandpas for a visit. They then flew back to Pendleton. With the press of business, expecting the new baby, and moving, time again passed very quickly. By June 13, we were in our "new" (1928 vintage) home on the ranch, enjoying country living.

Ryan Daniel arrived on the fifteenth. We were incredibly pleased when the doctor declared him fit as a fiddle. It is truly a blessing to welcome a healthy baby. Kay appreciated coming directly home from the hospital, especially in view of the earlier difficulties Robin had experienced.

Ryan
Man of Distinction

"It is well with the man who deals generously and lends, who conducts his affairs with justice" (Psalm 112:5, ESV).

One of the most enjoyable things each of us does is making plans. Often excitement and anticipation of future events are almost as enjoyable as the event itself. Having Ryan in our family has been a privilege and continuing joy. The energy level of little boys is so much greater than little girls'; it does not take long to appreciate the contrast. Our plans for having one boy and one girl were complete! We now had our perfect family. (We thought!)

Shortly thereafter, Robin started to have rectal problems again. By August, she was having so much difficulty we needed to take her back to Portland for additional surgery, this time, to remove scar tissue from earlier surgeries. The doctors assured us of solving the problem. It was not solved! Just after returning home, we were extremely disappointed to discover that, instead of the problem being solved, it was worse than ever.

Robin became so constipated it required a doctor's assistance to unplug her.

We were beginning to have serious doubts. At this point, we wondered what God's plan really was. How could a seemingly simple problem have continued to go from bad to worse? It was beginning to seem like Robin was spending more time in hospital beds than her own. Quite frankly, we were very frustrated. We were having feelings of anger toward God. How was it possible He would allow a small child to go through so much? Especially ours.

Additionally, our total situation was creating a great deal of stress. I was feeling pressure from the everyday problems of running the agency while trying to keep up with the ranch operation. Kay was under constant strain, caring for a new baby and dealing with Robin's continuing medical situation. We were not particularly happy with the way things were going. Both of us began to feel God had lost interest in our situation. After about a month, we were at the point of "Lord, this is it, we've had it."

God was there. We just did not realize it, nor did we imagine what was coming. He is always available to help those who love Him, but He usually waits until we are willing to let Him. Shortly afterward, God led us to an outstanding doctor in Seattle. After examining Robin, he knew precisely what the problem was and how to correct it. God's leading is often difficult to explain. However, without our knowing it, He was preparing us for much more serious problems to come. We discovered later, as you will see, just how important this was.

The doctor scheduled yet another surgery for early December when he would make the necessary corrections. We were finally finished with that problem.

Our family had a wonderful Christmas in 1971. Robin was two and quite the little mother to her little brother, Ryan. The holiday season really seemed to sparkle as we rejoiced over Christ's birth. We felt especially blessed with how God had answered our prayers. It was a very thankful and joyous time.

The kids were really growing. Robin's rectal difficulties did not return. I was spending more time on the road, traveling over Eastern Oregon on agency business. It was becoming increasingly harder to divide my time between insurance and ranching. The company began having questions about this also. By June, the time had come I left the agency, and we became full-time ranchers.

Robin began having a persistent bladder infection. For a period of about three months, she was on and off antibiotics. When the prescription would run out, the infection would flare up again. Our local doctor decided we should take her to a urologist for additional tests. He recommended a specialist in Walla Walla, Washington, and made the necessary arrangements.

The urologist scheduled a retrograde pyelogram. It was necessary for him to anesthetize her, resulting in a one-day hospitalization. Test results clearly indicated one of her kidneys was very badly contaminated. Having this infection over a period had destroyed the tissue. It would need to be removed. The doctor hastened to add, "It is not uncommon for a person to have only one kidney. We can live a normal life on approximately 10 percent of the kidney function available to us. With our modern-day processed foods and a well-balanced diet, our kidneys do not have to work awfully hard."

Continuing, the doctor also gave us a brief description of what our kidneys do, explaining very concisely how this complex organ is needed: "The most important function, of course, is filtering the blood. The fluid produces urine, carries the wastes out of the body. Also, the kidney produces a hormone that controls the manufacture of red blood cells. And it acts as a buffer, helping keep our blood pressure normal."

Honestly, we did not know what to think. As we discussed the situation, we felt it would be best to get a second opinion. Not that we doubted the doctor's judgment, we needed to assure ourselves of the necessity of another operation. We called the doctor who had completed the rectal revision, and he suggested a pediatric urologist in Seattle. In July, we went over for a follow-up examination. The urologist scheduled another retrograde pyelogram for October 23. Again, Robin would have to be anesthetized. His recommendation was to proceed with the surgery to remove the damaged kidney if the results of this second test were the same as before. We agreed with the doctor's assessment.

This seemed like the best course of action. We committed it to the Lord, trusting Him for the outcome. The doctor again confirmed what we had learned about being able to live a full life on one kidney.

October is an enjoyable time of year in Eastern Oregon. The long hot, busy days of summer begin to fade as the fall season arrives. That year, the harvest had been completed; the fall wheat crops were seeded. It was no problem taking a few days off. We drove over to the Nelsons (Kay's parents) for a short visit before continuing to Seattle. Ryan would stay with the grandparents while we were with Robin during her hospital stay.

2

More Problems

We checked her in the night of the twenty-second. The next morning, we were with her when they came to take her for the test. She went into the surgical unit at about 7:00 a.m. Her doctor indicated a nurse would let us know the results at around nine o'clock.

This gave us a little time to do some exploring. We found the cafeteria and ate breakfast. In the past two and a half years, we had been in several hospitals. Kay and I marveled at the quality of the people and care here at Children's Orthopedic: so many children with a multitude of varying medical problems, and yet there seemed to be a positive, caring attitude among the staff, nurses, and doctors.

One of the staff showed us their new care-by-parent unit. Here a parent moves in with their child, depending on the condition, and takes over duties such as meals, bathing, dressing, and giving medicine. This is less threatening to the child, and the parent is better able to understand the whys and therefores. We also visited with other parents who had children in the hospital and, in general, felt a real sense of reassurance everything possible would be done for our child.

At about nine o'clock, a nurse came with the doctor's report. Test results confirmed the need to remove the damaged kidney. The surgical team was going ahead as planned; Robin should be back in her room about noon.

We spent the rest of the morning taking care of financial details at the business office. While employed at the agency, we had exceptionally good medical coverage. Leaving, I had converted this to an individual family policy. This coverage was not as comprehensive; however, we felt it was adequate for the time being. At noon, we were back, waiting for Robin's return.

By four o'clock, we were becoming genuinely concerned. Robin was still not out of surgery. The duty nurses were not able to provide much information other than to tell us there had been some complications. This kind of generalization leaves a lot of unanswered questions—the type you do not even know how to ask. Kay and I began feeling very desperate and lonely. We were praying it was not serious.

Around five o'clock, ten hours after Robin had gone for the retest, a team of doctors came down the corridor, still dressed in their surgical gowns. I will never forget the look of exhaustion and discouragement written across the faces of those men. They took Kay and me into a waiting room. Each appeared to be literally drained, physically and emotionally, and was at a loss for words.

We were quite surprised to see Dr. Bill. He had performed the final rectal surgery and, to our knowledge, was not involved with the kidney problem. It was, however, reassuring to see someone we knew. He became the spokesman for the group and sat us down to explain exactly what complications had arisen.

This doctor will always stand out in our memory. He is an extremely gifted person in his ability to explain the most complicated of problems in such a way even a child can fully comprehend. The doctor took a large piece of paper from an examination table, a black felt-tip pen to diagram out in life size exactly what had happened.

"Now," Dr. Bill said, "if you were to look at this drawing as an X-ray picturing the inside of the body, you would see here—" pointing, "in the lower back, appearing to be attached to the backbone, two objects. They almost look like small balloons. These are our kidneys. Your daughters appeared in the X-ray just as I have drawn, entirely normal-looking situation."

He continued, "During the exam, retrograde pyelogram, this one," pointing out the right kidney, "became enlarged several times its normal size, indicating the tissue inside the organ had been destroyed. It would need to be removed." Dr. Bill then drew a large circle on the paper with two smaller circles inside. "This is a cross section at the base of the kidney to show how it should have one artery and one vein used to move the blood into and out of the filter (kidney) to remove the wastes. These impurities are then flushed into the bladder." He drew a line down from each kidney and labeled them ureters. He then added many smaller circles inside the large one. "When the surgeon removed the diseased kidney and turned it to look at the cross section, he was confronted with multiple arteries and veins (seventeen to be exact) instead of the usual one of each."

The others nodded in agreement.

"He very quickly determined he had removed a portion of one horseshoe-shaped kidney, all she had. The portion that remained, while not as badly infected, became instantly contaminated when the cut was made. Additionally, compounding things: there were multiple ureters (tubes that carry the wastes to the bladder). There was no way of knowing. On the X-rays, the backbone masked the base of the horseshoe-shaped kidney mass, making it appear like there were two normal organs. Also, everything is very tiny in a small body."

It was a totally impossible situation. Finding this unusual condition, the surgeon immediately called for assistance. The group of surgeons had spent the rest of the day trying every conceivable way to salvage a portion of the kidney mass. A transplant surgeon had been called in. He had thought it might be possible to graft a small piece back in hopes of salvaging something. Finally, there were no alternatives left. The surgeon removed the balance of the tissue and closed Robin up without any kidney function.

At this point, the team excused themselves. They left the room. Kay and I were in total shock! A flood of questions came into our minds, disbelief, confusion: it is hard to remember what went on around us for the rest of the evening. However, shortly after, a doctor returned and explained to us he was involved with the kidney dialysis unit. He would try to answer our questions. We knew little about kidneys and less about dialysis.

The doctor began, "Dialysis is the process of separating wastes from the blood. This is necessary when the kidneys either stop functioning or are removed. There are two types used. Hemodialysis is when the blood is taken out of the body, cleansed by a filtering process, and returned. Peritoneal dialysis is a different procedure in which a warm solution is put into the abdomen in contact with the peritoneum, a thin membrane covering the organs, then through osmosis, the impurities and waste fluid are drawn out of the blood."

It should be noted that this was in 1971. While kidney disease had been recognized for some time, dialysis and kidney transplants were still in their infancy. Successful transplanting of kidneys in adults had only recently been done. Emergency peritoneal dialysis was routine, for instance, with heart-attack patients whose kidneys had stopped; however, application of this type for chronic (long-term) patients was just being explored. They were using chronic hemodialysis on adults successfully. They had no way to provide for children with chronic kidney disease.

He patiently continued with his explanation, "Hemodialysis, while the more efficient process, is not possible at this time of use with small children. Their veins are too tiny for continual use. Peritoneal dialysis, on the other hand, might work. However, we have not used it successfully on small children. In fact, if we are to use long-term peritoneal dialysis on your daughter, she will be one of the youngest ever." He noted they were currently trying it on another child, Chris (who subsequently died shortly after). Additionally, they knew of one other attempt at the University of Minnesota Medical School. The child there was older than Robin, however, about the same size. They were having relatively good success with teenage children, depending on what other medical problems they had.

He then stated, "Chronic dialysis, either at a kidney center or at home, is merely a way to keep a person alive. As we have no experience with small children, it will be impossible to predict what long-term effects this will have. To date, small children have not been transplanted."

By this time, Kay and I were totally confused. It had barely been an hour since finding out Robin did not have any kidney function. We had heard the word "dialysis" somewhere. It was something that happened to other people. What we knew about it was absolutely nothing. It seemed like our minds were paralyzed. It was unreal. We were not really having this conversation. At his point, not knowing what else to say, I asked, "What would you recommend, doctor?"

He paused, putting my question aside, while he talked about the severe psychological and emotional strain dialysis puts on the patient and their family. He related very serious disturbances and other problems. Then he went on about how they did not think children would continue growing. Also, they did not feel present machines being tried for peritoneal dialysis were adequate. And lastly, besides these problems, there would be tremendous financial costs.

Then, without showing any emotion, he answered my question, "If I were you, I would just let her go. The costs are extremely high in terms of emotional strain and expense."

I looked at him and said, "You mean to just let her die?"

"Yes," he continued, "you are young and can have other children. Knowing what others with older children have endured, I think that could be best."

We could feel the tension building. Kay and I were shocked, becoming agitated and unsettled. Kay began crying. We could not believe what we had just heard the doctor say. I do not recall whether I stood up or continued sitting, but I replied almost immediately, "No, God gave us this little girl; we won't let her die! We will do everything we can for her."

This was the response he wanted. As quickly as the tension had swelled, it melted away. He assured us we would need that kind of determination. He also made a commitment to Kay and me of their support, medical and technical, in doing everything possible to help Robin. The doctor left, saying he would be back in the morning.

Robin was just returning to her room. It had now been over twelve hours since we had seen her. We spent the rest of the night and many hours over the next few days wrestling with ourselves and God. Questions kept moving through our minds: *How is it possible for a loving God to allow a child to lose so much? Does God really love us? We say we are Christians; what does it matter? Can we get through all the problems and hurdles, many of which we do not even have enough knowledge of to understand? Is there any such thing as God's will? Can God's plan for our lives really include disabling our child, making her dependent on some kind of machine? Why, God?*

While we were struggling with these personal battles, as is often the case in a crisis situation, the urgency and demands of just getting from one day to the next kept our minds and bodies drained. However, during this time, we were to uncover and rediscover valuable truths about this God we say we serve.

For you to understand, we have to go back to the beginning. God made man perfect. He also made a perfect environment (earth) for man to live in. God also gave man the power of choice (free will). God's perfect plan is for everything, including man, to worship and honor Him. However, the first man and woman rejected God's plan and chose to discover the knowledge of good and evil on their own when they ate of the tree, which God had forbidden. At that point, God punished man by instituting death, both physical and spiritual.

> The judgment followed one sin and brought condemnation, but the gift followed many trespasses and brought justification. For if, by the trespass of the one man, death reigned through that one man, how much more will those who receive God's abundant provision of grace and the gift of righteousness reign through the one man, Jesus Christ.
>
> Romans 5:16–17

So, what God intended for a perfect world and perfect people was made imperfect. We are all going to die physically; we have no choice. All humanity is in the same condition. Suffering, disease, and decay of our physical bodies are all part of the process leading to physical death. God called this the sin of disobedience.

"There is no difference [...], for all have sinned and fall short of the glory of God" (Romans 3:22–23).

When the first man broke the perfect relationship with God, a sinful nature became part of his being. We, all of humanity, inherited this sinful nature. God was not causing Robin to suffer. These medical problems are part of the process leading to physical death.

"For he does not willingly bring affliction or grief to the children of men" (Lamentations 3:33).

We are also dead spiritually. However, God provided a way through Christ's shed blood to overcome this condition.

"For the wages of sin is death, but the gift of God is eternal life in Christ Jesus our Lord" (Romans 6:23).

Kay and I had accepted God's gift, His Son, as our personal Savior and Lord. Knowing this, we could claim His promise.

"And we know that in all things God works for the good of those who love Him, who have been called according to His purpose" (Romans 8:28).

3

Pritoneal Dialysis

Robin was being kept alive using a jerry-rigged apparatus the hospital made up to perform the peritoneal dialysis. This was a two-burner electric hot plate, a set of timers out of a stop-and-go traffic light, a small rubber hose pump, two electric pressure valves, an empty twenty-liter jug, and a twenty-liter jug of dialysis solution. The hot plate with the full jug, timers, valves, and pump was on a hospital cart pulled up by the bed. The empty jug sat on the floor.

Every Monday, Wednesday, and Friday, the lab at the University of Washington Hospital would make up a batch of solution. Then, using sterilized rubber hoses, they would "hook" Robin up. For the next twelve hours, the system would pump small amounts of solution into her abdomen. After approximately ten minutes, while osmosis would draw a small amount of fluid with wastes out of the blood, a pressure valve on the tubing would open, allowing this liquid to drain out of the abdomen into the empty jug. Then the cycle would start over. The process would be repeated, seventy or so times, during the night.

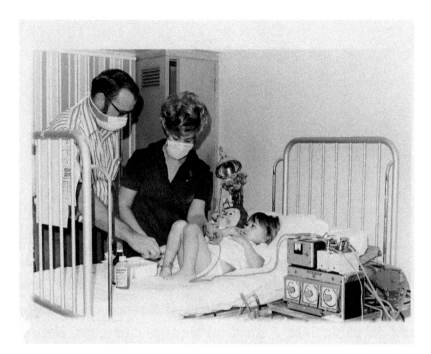

The doctor had been right about questioning the equipment available for peritoneal dialysis! However, the process worked very well. During the "run," Robin would lose between two and three pounds, the same fluids and wastes your kidneys would normally remove. She was a particularly good patient, never complaining, and accepted the situation as necessary. She was even able to sleep.

They had surgically implanted a small tube in Robin's abdomen. This was a special catheter designed for small children, the Hickman catheter, designed and developed by Dr. Hickman, Robin's doctor! It allowed her to be "hooked up" to the machine. When she came off the machine, the catheter was capped off.

We were put in room 328 of the new care-by-patent unit! This allowed us to be with Robin and learn as much as possible about dialysis. They began training us to take over operating the apparatus and keep up the medical records. Our hope was to eventually be able to take her and the machine home.

We were from out of state, from Oregon. Our health insurance was used up, and in 1971, Social Security had not yet recognized chronic kidney dialysis for benefits. Oregon did have a kidney association, which was doing adult hemodialysis in conjunction with the University of Oregon Medical School. However, their program did not include peritoneal dialysis. Also, they were not working with children. On the other hand, Northwest Kidney Association at Swedish Medical Center in Seattle was doing work with home peritoneal dialysis using a cumbersome machine built by Colb Company for adults.

Because we were nonresidents, Northwest Kidney turned down our request for inclusion into their program. Their rules did allow for supplying out-of-state home dialysis patients, except on a private-pay basis. This required a $20,000 deposit. We did not have $20,000!

Our situation seemed impossible. Had God abandoned us? No, He was there, ready to do what He promised as soon as we were willing to leave it in His hands. One of the things God's Word talks about repeatedly is love, the kind of giving love that neither wants nor demands anything in return. Without love, nothing else matters. God's love for us was so great that He gave His only Son to die for us.

"And now these three remain: faith, hope, and love. But the greatest of these is love" (1 Corinthians 13:13).

One of the ways God shows His love is through people. We were overwhelmed with a demonstration of this love through people across the nation. After hearing of our desperate situation, two members of the local Kiwanis club and a group of local Pendleton businessmen organized an effort to try raising the necessary funds.

The owner of a local radio station kicked off with the fund drive early in the morning of Friday, November 17, with a daylong radiothon. Within minutes, a long-haul trucker pulled off the freeway, came into the station, and handed them a one-hundred-dollar bill. By day's end, over $6,700 had been collected or pledged for Robin.

Our situation was also put on the national wire service, and people from New Jersey, Florida, and across the nation began responding. During the evening, one of the men from the Kiwanis club placed a call to radio station KGO, San Francisco, and many of the midnight listeners sent contributions. Early the next morning, Inez Harris, a blind lady from West Sacramento, California, having heard about Robin on KGO, called Herb Jepko at KSL radio in Salt Lake City, and the Nitecaps from all over started sending in one dollar each, including schoolchildren.

Dear Sir, I am a Nitecap. There are thousands of us that listen and belong to the Herb Jepco Nitecap show ever night from KSL Salt Lake, Utah and while waiting for that program to come on at Midnite, I was listening to the KGO show, When I heard your plea for funds for little Robin Petrik. So had a friend call the Nitecap program and repeat what I heard on KGO, if all of the Nitecaps come through with a dollar you

*should have mor than enough for little Robin. I am blind so
please excuse mistakes.*
May little Robin have Many Birthdays in the future.
Sincerely. Inez Harris

Churches and sorority groups also had projects to help. Some classes gave up their gift exchanges and sent in the money normally spent for those items.

Miraculously, almost overnight, there was more than enough to solve the current financial problems. We were able to give God the praise for how He uses ordinary people in an incredibly unique way to accomplish His will. The Robin Petrik fund drive raised $11,000 to cover our initial expenses and make preparations for her return home.

A lady of Bellevue, Washington, instead of sending money, sent something Robin understood: a dolly that carried a tiny red purse. She also sent something else Robin understood, a short letter saying, "all my love."

"There's just no way we can adequately express our gratitude and thanks to all the wonderful people who have responded," Kay said. Not in words, perhaps. But gratitude certainly showed when we, the Petriks, smiled at Robin.

God does answer prayer. The response may not be in a way we expect, and He always answers in His time; the answer comes through, loud and clear. We must also remember there are times when God is silent. Waiting is the most difficult situation to be in. It was extremely hard for Kay and me since we did not know what was going to happen. I must confess we were not very patient. Sometimes not receiving an answer is definitely a "no."

Robin responded very well to this new lifestyle. She accepted the machine and conditions much more quickly than her mom and dad. The strength and courage of our daughter were remarkable. Her attitude not only helped us but was, I feel, used by God to bolster and encourage our faith.

We spent a total of forty days at the hospital. During this time, we were learning about dialysis and training the operation of the machine. Slowly, we began to take over these responsibilities. Kay was learning to be a nutritionist and nurse. It was essential to monitor Robin's diet. Also, Kay and I both had to understand the correct sterile procedures for "hooking" the tubing up to her. Naturally, it was necessary to know each of the different medications. Additionally, my responsibility was to properly maintain and operate the equipment. Robin was the perfect patient. Her grasp and willingness to accept the situation amazed and inspired us.

Early in December, we were ready to go home. It would be different because we had to center our lives around a machine, but we felt with God's continued help, we could manage. We visited with the doctor before leaving. He felt if Robin adjusted well to dialysis, she would stay on it until her early teens. By which time, providing she kept growing, they would consider a transplant. The doctor also emphasized several times the pioneering nature of her treatment. There were just so many unknowns it was impossible to predict what would happen in the future. His parting comment was, "But I am confident you and Kay will do an excellent job."

Robin's third birthday and holidays were a joyous celebration, possible only because of the love and generosity manifested by hundreds and hundreds of ordinary people. She received so many cards and letters it was hard to imagine the number of hearts touched by one little girl.

Despite the machine routine, we were delighted to be at home together as a family. That Christmas, more than any other, reminded us in a unique way of the importance of having the right priorities. Without a personal relationship with God's Son, whose birth we celebrated, and our dependence on Him, could we have endured the seemingly impossible series of events over the past three years? Our disappointments and frustrations were being overcome with a new sense of hope and faith in the knowledge that indeed God is in charge.

We were learning a great deal. God was showing us the awesome responsibility we have as parents to love and care for the children we bring into this world. He was teaching us that these children are not ours; they belong to Him. He holds us responsible, during the fleeting period of time we care for them, to bring them up in His nurture and admonition.

"A Child of Mine"

"I'll lend you for a little time a child of mine," He said,
"For you to love the while she lives and mourn for
     when she's dead.
It may be six, or seven years, or twenty-two or three,
But will you, till I call her back, take care of her for
     Me?

She'll bring her charm to gladden you, and should
her stay be brief,
You'll have her lovely memories as solace for your
grief.
I cannot promise she will stay, since all on earth
returns.
But there are lessons taught down there I want this
child to learn.
I've looked the wide world over in My search for
teachers true,
And from the throngs that crowd life's lanes, I have
selected you.
How will you give her all your love, nor think the labor vain?
Nor hate Me when I come to call, to take her back
again?"
I fancied that I heard them say, "Dear Lord, thy will
be done!
For all the joy Thy child shall bring, the risk of grief
we'll run,
We'll shelter her with tenderness, we'll love her while
we may,
And for the happiness we've known, forever grateful
stay.
But should the angels call for her much sooner than
we've planned,
We'll brave the bitter grief that comes and try to
understand."[1]

Kay and I had not realized so many children have medical problems. Friends with children often had minor medical crises, but, I think, we were like most people who know little about major medical difficulties. Robin's earlier anal problem, while serious, had seemed to us more a correctable situation than a catastrophe. The more we became involved, the easier it was to empathize with other families going through similar experiences. We developed strong ties with some of these families.

Having a daughter on chronic kidney dialysis was a learning experience. Our lives began to take shape around this every-other-night routine. At first, she had been on the machine Monday, Wednesday, and Friday nights; however, this had been changed to every other night. She was retaining too much fluid in the extra day over the weekend.

We connected Robin to the machine at bedtime, monitored both her and the system during that night, and disconnected her the next morning. Then the machine would be cleaned and sterilized in readiness for another run. In addition, Kay maintained an elaborate set of daily records. These included weight gains and losses, periodic blood pressure readings, general appearance and condition, food values and intake, medications, and other necessary information needed by the doctors and us.

Besides removing wastes from the blood, the kidneys are a key member of the bodily system directly or indirectly influencing distinct functions. These included the complex interactions affected with levels of calcium, potassium, and sodium. Low levels of calcium in children can cause problems with growth and bone development, including teeth. Elevated levels of sodium directly increase blood pressure and can cause heart problems. A slight variance in potassium will cause death. What complicates matters even more is that, during the peritoneal dialysis run, a great deal of protein is inadvertently removed. Diet becomes an essential part of the chronic problem. A no-salt, low potassium, high-protein menu, while possible, is extremely bland and tasteless. Preparing three exciting meals every day was a very exasperating challenge for Kay.

Robin had blood drawn each week at the lab in Pendleton. The results indicated how well the total job was being done. If you consider the complexity of the situation and that we resided 250 miles from her doctor, Kay did an outstanding job keeping everything in balance. Through her selfless dedication to detail and willingness to accept these new responsibilities, Robin did very well. Peritonitis, an infection inside the abdomen that can inhibit dialysis and later cause transplant difficulties, was a constant concern. This was never a problem, even though Kay opened the catheter (tube in Robin's abdomen) every other day. Also, Robin's blood chemistries never varied outside the acceptable ranges—a real credit to both mother and daughter.

We were still using the old hospital machine. Every two weeks, I went to Seattle for a new supply of twenty-liter jugs containing the dialysis fluid. Also, I picked up other freshly sterilized supplies. I would drive up and back in one day (a 500-mile round trip). Each time I would visit with our supporting staff. We were anxious to be brought up-to-date on the latest developments on the new machine. It was being developed by Drake-Willock, a company in Portland, in cooperation with the Veterans Administration Hospital in Seattle.

By June, the new machine was finally ready for production. I was scheduled to spend two weeks at the VA Hospital training on the Drake-Willock unit. My good technician and teacher put me through the program in less than a week. While the old hospital apparatus had used a large quantity of premixed solution, the new machine proportioned a small amount of a concentrated mixture with water as it entered the abdomen. A Colligan representative designed a system to purify and sterilize our well water. University Hospital would make up the two-liter bottles of concentrate for us since it would be a while before it was available commercially. The new machine was much more dependable and easier to use. It would be a blessing.

Drake-Willock told us the cost of the new machine would be $17,500. We did not have $17,500. We were crushed; we knew the new machine would be a huge blessing, but...our faith was again being tested.

"'Have faith in God,' Jesus answered. [...] 'Therefore I tell you, whatever you ask for in prayer, believe that you have received it, and it will be yours'" (Mark 11:22–24).

We prayed, asking in faith, believing.

"That sum almost certainly will be realized," said the two members of the Pendleton Kiwanis club, which originally publicized Robin's plight. Proceeds of a basketball game between Blue Mountain Community College and the Whitman College jayvees gave the proceeds of their game to Robin—the game netted $125. The Pendleton Shrine Club raffled a beef and raised $1,500 for Robin. A man from Toms River, New Jersey, sent a check after reading of Robin's plight in the Newark Star-Ledger. The Valby Lutheran Church in Ione sent a Thanksgiving offering of $55.88. Collections, Inc., of Portland gave $438 in lieu of Christmas presents to clients. And so many others!

Within one week, the community of Pendleton, surrounding ranchers, KAO (Kidney Association of Oregon), and people around the nation contributed over $15,000 for the new machine.

Robin's fund at $15,000

The fund for Robin Petrik, the little girl whose kidneys were removed during surgery in mid-October, has climbed to $15,000.

Robin, who will be 3 on Dec. 24, is on a dialysis (artificial kidney) machine loaned by the University of Washington Medical School. The fund drive was started to enable Robin's parents, Mr. and Mrs. Robert Petrik, who reside some 15 miles west of Pendleton, to acquire a new dialysis machine.

It has been estimated that purchase of the machine and its operation for three years — at which time a transplant may be possible — will cost $17,500.

That sum almost certainly will be realized, said Bob Russell and Perry Daboling. Russell and Daboling, members of the Pendleton Kiwanis Club, of which Petrik also is a member, originally publicized Robin's plight.

Daboling reported today that 200 of 2,500 "Christmas for Robin" buttons had been sold for $1 each and it was hoped the balance of the buttons would be purchased by Christmas.

Proceeds of a basketball game last Friday night between Blue Mountain Community College and the Whitman College jayvees will be turned over to the fund for Robin. The game netted $125.

The Pendleton Shrine Club raffled a beef and raised $1,500 for Robin.

Mr. and Mrs. Hank Pedersen of Meacham planned to raffle a 6-month-old stallion colt and give the proceeds to Robin. When they learned that sufficient funds apparently were going to be contributed, they decided they would give the colt to the girl.

Does God answer our prayers when it is within His will? Kay and I would say without question—He does what He says!

Drake-Willock accepted the funds raised! We installed the new equipment in July. The Drake-Willock model I brought home was one of the very first to be assembled. It did not even have a serial number. The old hospital unit had served us well; however, we felt very blessed to have a new, more reliable, and advanced machine. This unit had a good monitoring system and was extremely reliable. If any unusual circumstance occurred, an alarm would sound, letting us know. We were now much more comfortable sleeping during the nights Robin was on the machine.

It was necessary for her to take twenty-five pills every day. Eighteen of these were the largest-size capsules available. This variety of medication helped compensate for some of the missing kidney functions. It was a daily battle of diet, machine, and pills.

Robin continued to be the ideal patient. We knew from observing her, as well as visiting with others (adults) on dialysis, that she never really felt good. Her energy level was extremely low. However, she never complained and handled the situation much better than the rest of us. Her patience seemingly extended into an understanding of what was involved. She willingly submitted herself to whatever was needed at a particular moment to overcome the crisis at hand. For instance, repeatedly, the lab technicians would be unable to find a vein. Without complaining, Robin would sit watching them poke and poke the needles until they could draw the necessary blood.

Her greatest joy was reading. She constantly challenged herself with more difficult books and puzzles. She also enjoyed playing school and nurse with her dolls and stuffed animals.

Naturally, her little brother was either a student or a patient depending on the concern at the moment.

Shortly before Christmas, we received a call from one of my Kiwanis friends. He asked if it would be all right to bring Robin a special gift. They had been contacted by a family whose young daughter had a very crippling disease. She would no longer be able to ride a horse. This incredibly special young lady wanted Robin to have her most prized possession, a yearling colt.

They had planned to auction the colt and give the proceeds to the new machine fund. But, finding out the necessary money had already been given, the girl wanted to give her colt to Robin as a Christmas present.

Clip Clop arrived a few days later. What a beautiful young animal! Robin named him after a horse from one of her favorite storybooks. He was a half-Arabian, half-Quarter horse, a beautiful dark sorrel with three white stockings and a star on his forehead. His mane and tail were black. He loved to prance around and show off. He and Robin would become pals.

Robin and the young girl never met; however, the empathy and love expressed were an extra special Christmas blessing.

Ryan had adjusted well. He fully accepted both the machine and his sister's condition. The only thing he never really understood was not being able to help "hook" Robin up. Because we had to do this procedure under sterile conditions, he was not allowed in her room during those few minutes. Being a determined lad, at times, he would beat on the door, all the while yelling at the top of his lungs. He was nowhere in sight by the time we could open the door.

Watermelons ripen early in this area. We decided to feast on some one evening before Robin went on the machine. This was a special treat for her because melons are high in potassium. We all enjoyed our special evening dessert. Kay and Robin went up to her room to get ready for the "run." Ryan and I had gone outside. Suddenly, Kay began screaming for me to come. I rushed into the house and up the stairs to find her trying to keep Robin from swallowing her tongue. She was having a seizure. We did not know what to do. We thought we had lost her when suddenly she came to herself and sat up. She had already turned blue.

We never determined what caused the seizure. They did a spinal tap and other tests without uncovering any specific problems. Also, they ruled out the possibility of too much watermelon triggering the incident. We only know it was a remarkably narrow escape from death for Robin. We felt God had intervened and kept her alive. We felt God's hand on our lives again.

God was continuing to teach Kay and me. Accepting ourselves and our situation was a difficult lesson to learn. We once again found ourselves questioning God and wishing somehow things could be different. Throughout the summer, we felt like we were under a great deal of pressure. The normal activities and routines of life and providing for a family with two small children can be difficult enough. Adding the extra responsibility of caring for a chronically ill child, we began to feel imprisoned with a seemingly unfair burden. As parents, we love our children and are willing to sacrifice for them. We understood this. However, we were constantly haunted by the questions, "Why our child, why us, Lord?" Why can't our life be normal like other families?

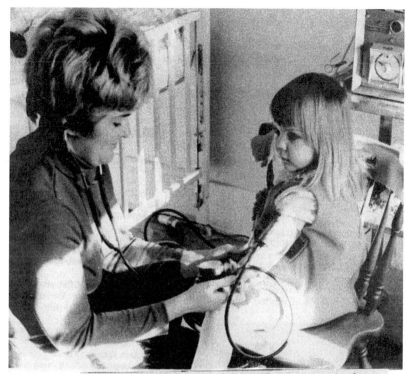

Three times daily, Kay must give Robin a check-up to make sure her body is functioning normally. Robin must use the peritoneal dialysis machine for 12 hours once every two days.

We realized death and suffering result from the first man rejecting God. The difficulty was in accepting this judgment when we experienced the outworking of it in our own child. We also knew He is merciful and loving because He subsequently provided the way, through Christ's shed blood, for us to be made spiritually right. Why then did He not make provisions for restoring our physical bodies as well?

The only way I can understand this is to accept the fact God is sovereign, absolute, perfect, and unchangeable. He created us in His image solely for us to serve and honor Him. He could have made "clones," people who would do nothing but His will.

However, their worship and honor would be meaningless. They would not have any choice. The perfection of God's plan is a matter of choice. When we choose to accept His plan, He then receives perfect honor and glory as well as our service. His judgment is also perfect.

We still kept asking, "But why, God?" Many times, God reveals His answers to our questions through His Word.

> We were under great pressure, far beyond our ability to endure, so that we despaired even of life. Indeed, in our hearts we felt the sentence of death. But this happened that we might not rely on ourselves but on God.
>
> 2 Corinthians 1:8–9

We can accept ourselves and our situation if we trust God. As we struggled through this difficult period, Romans, chapter eight, became one of our favorite and comforting passages of Scripture.

As we learned to accept Robin's condition, we were also able to accept dependence on the machine as our new lifestyle. Our lives could be normal. This was our circumstance.

We decided it might be a good idea to start Robin in preschool. She was anxious to learn. One mention of school—she was ready to go. We were not confident about putting her in a group situation. However, we felt it would be good for her to be around more children. We knew she would be on dialysis for a long time, probably well into the elementary-school years.

We enrolled her in the Pendleton Presbyterian Nursery School. She loved it! She was thrilled with the coloring and other learning activities. It was amazing, but the other preschoolers never realized she had a problem. Mrs. Brede, her teacher, marveled at how quickly Robin learned and fit in.

We began to feel the holiday spirit. Robin enjoyed the Christmas party at the preschool. She really delighted her parents. At the annual Elks Club Christmas party, she could not leave Santa alone. Holding his hand, she talked his leg off. What she wanted was a doll, "Baby Chrissy," and her very own desk to do her schoolwork at.

Between birthday and Christmas, Robin got all her wishes. We were especially thankful for God's patience with us. Coming to the realization that, through Him, all things are possible, we had a much stronger feeling about the true peace and joy this special season represented.

Nineteen seventy-three had been a real learning experience for us. Finally, we were beginning to accept our situation. (We were still in the same prison, but turning our circumstances over to God, we sensed more freedom from those feelings.) Nineteen seventy-four would be a good year, in fact, a pivotal one for Robin and ourselves.

Robin continued to excel both as a patient and preschooler. We were taking her back to Seattle about every three months for a checkup. As the doctor suspected, Robin was not growing. However, her general health was excellent, and she was responding very well to being on dialysis. Dr. Hickman was always glad to see us. He attributed a great deal of her continued success to Nurse Kay and "good country living."

At Easter time, Grandma and Grandpa Petrik came for a visit. The kids always enjoy the special attention only grandparents can give. A few weeks after they left, our Country Extension Office was looking for families to host visiting diplomats from Washington, DC. The program was sponsored by a foundation back East. Their goal was to familiarize members of the foreign diplomatic staff with "real America." We decided to be a host family despite the machine routine. Our diplomat came from the tiny African country of Dahomey (modern-day Benin). He was a black man and stayed with us for several days. Within a short time, Robin was referring to him as "the other grandpa." All of us really enjoyed his stay. Being introduced to a different culture was a valuable experience.

Robin immensely enjoyed her part in the spring nursery-school program. She was not bashful in the least. We discovered, much to our delight, she loved to perform. She was proud of her certificate upon completing the first preschool year. She did not like the thought of waiting until fall to continue with her schooling.

In June, we celebrated Ryan's birthday. He was growing fast and, sizewise, had almost caught up with his sister. Both were large at birth. This had been a plus for Robin. She was in the ninety-eighth percentile for her age group when she lost her kidney; now, she was only in the fiftieth percentile.

Early in summer, we went to Seattle for a checkup. En route and while at the hospital, we visited several of our "kidney friends." We stopped in Yakama and visited a family with two older children who were both experiencing kidney failure, anticipating dialysis in the near future.

God's Word teaches us about the positive aspects of suffering and the trials we endure. This enables us to minister more effectively to others who are experiencing similar problems:

"And the God of all comfort, who comforts us in all our troubles, so that we can comfort those in any trouble with the comfort we ourselves have received from God" (2 Corinthians 1:3–4).

We find much greater joy and satisfaction during the good times, having experienced difficult ones and being able to share with others.

This was an important year in the Northwest. Spokane was hosting the 1974 World Exposition. During the past two years, we had not left the ranch except for medical appointments and preschool. No vacations. We were anxious to get away for a break and decided this event would be an exciting time (two hundred miles away). It might be possible if we left early, after Robin came off the machine, to return in time for the next run. We would spend one night in a Spokane motel. The only risks involved might be an accident or car trouble.

In September, we followed through on our plans and had a fantastic time. We rented two strollers, and the kids really enjoyed visiting the exhibits of the different countries. Kay's and my taste buds thrilled at sampling the good ethnic foods. Typical of children, Robin and Ryan did not want to eat anything with a foreign-sounding name. This solved the dietary predicament. While Mom and Dad were eating salty, seasoned foods, they enjoyed the carnival rides. The change in scenery was very refreshing. We did not encounter any difficulties.

Before we knew it, Thanksgiving was approaching and it was time for another checkup back in Seattle. As Dr. Hickman was reviewing the test results with us, we were totally unprepared for his prognosis!

We had gotten to know her doctor very well. He had given us a great deal of help and support through very tough times. He always made himself available to us via phone (any time, day or night) for any questions or advice when we could not get things done correctly. Doc, as we affectionately called him, is, without a doubt, the most dedicated physician we will ever know. His patience, loving and helpful attitude are a tribute to himself and the medical community.

4

Kidney Transplant

We were prepared to maintain Robin on dialysis until she was twelve or thirteen years old. This would be the earliest they would attempt a transplant. After reviewing the checkup results and her progress over the past two years, Doc looked up at us with a slight grin and asked, "Are you ready to go for a transplant?"

We were overjoyed! We could not believe our ears as he explained about recent developments making it possible to consider a transplant much sooner than expected. The transplant surgeon had developed a new serum for suppressing rejection immediately following a transplant. Also, the newer drugs for continued immunosuppressant therapy were not likely to interfere with normal growth, the anticipated problems of getting a child through puberty. (An interesting sidenote: I love horses, his wife was also a horse lover. He had used some of her horses in the experimental development of the new serum!)

Both Kay and I were possible candidates for becoming the donor. They had both of us complete the donor workup evaluations. We finished these during the next few days. The transplant surgeries were scheduled for January 22, 1975!

We returned home in time to get ready for Robin's fifth birthday. Kay and Robin's teacher planned a celebration at preschool with her pals. The kids all had a grand time but mostly talked about what they wanted for Christmas. It did not seem to matter to Robin; she just enjoyed having a party.

We celebrated Christmas with a special joy, realizing not only had God given us the gift of a new life through His Son whose birth we celebrated, but in answer to our prayers, He had given Robin the gift of an opportunity for a new physical life. The holiday season centered around getting ready for the transplant. It seemed as if time passed quickly.

Shortly after the first of the year, the doctors notified us of the results from the donor workups. They chose Kay as her match scored slightly higher than mine: A C– for her and a D+ for me (on their compatibility scoring system). Both of us were willing to donate an organ. If the first transplant failed, mine would be in reserve. A perfect match, A+, would only be possible with identical twins. Most cadavers (organs from someone deceased) would score on the lowest end of the scale.

There had been much continuing publicity about Robin. The news service was quick to pick up on the impending transplant. Everyone was concerned and anxious for her to be healthy again! And, if successful, Robin would be the youngest child to ever be transplanted! One dear lady from Birmingham, Alabama, had called and written faithfully since the first fund drive. This lady, whose husband was a state senator, exemplified the love so many continuously expressed. It was exciting for Kay to report to her the transplant had been scheduled.

It was overwhelming to hear the number of people who offered to give a kidney. We were especially touched by letters from inmates at different prisons writing to offer one of their kidneys. Relatives and others were also willing; living nonrelatives were not acceptable as donors, and of relatives, only immediate family over eighteen were considered under special circumstances.

The doctors could not predict how long Robin would be hospitalized. They suggested we should plan to stay in Seattle afterward for a period so they could monitor the new kidney. Grandma and Grandad Nelson would be there with us for moral support and to help with Ryan. Because of these considerations, we felt it was best to rent an apartment nearby.

Kay and Robin checked into University Hospital a week before the scheduled transplant. This was necessary to finish up last-minute tests and make final preparation for the double surgery. Kay would be operated on first. A doctor would remove her kidney, and while this was being completed, the transplant doctor would be preparing Robin.

I mentioned earlier the transplant surgeon (the same surgeon) had tried in vain to graft back a portion of the inadvertently removed kidney. This was a definite plus because he was able to plan the surgery in detail before beginning. He already knew the right iliac artery was absent, which allowed him to proceed directly with emphasis on the left side. He did not encounter any difficulties. However, he did find it necessary to remove her spleen. Then, after fashioning a pocket for the new organ on the forward wall of the abdomen, he affixed Kay's freshly removed kidney, completing the hookup with the remaining iliac artery and renal vein; the new kidney immediately started producing urine! It was already working before the doctor closed Robin up. Truly a miracle!

We often hear or read about the miracles of modern medicine. I wonder if we really realize what this means. God in His sovereignty and through His provision has given to man gifts of knowledge and skill. Using these talents, man is literally able to perform miracles. It is puzzling why so many people refuse to give God credit. They fail to recognize His enabling power and authority. Jesus touched on this very subject when He talked about the rich man and Lazarus: "They will not be convinced even if someone rises from the dead" (Luke 16:31).

Kay responded very well after her surgery. We had been forewarned she would have a great deal of discomfort, which she did. This resulted from her surgeon's policy of not using any pain medicines! His primary reasoning was that they can mask other symptoms, which, if unnoticed, can lead to complications. Additionally, without pain medicine, he assured her she would be out of the hospital within five days. She managed somehow, and as predicted, he released her on the fifth day.

Robin's new kidney continued to work flawlessly. However, she did experience some surgery-provoked problems. For some reason, over a period of about three weeks following the transplant, they were unable to control a spiking fever. Finally, it did level off but remained slightly above normal. At this point in time, Robin was able to leave the ward for short periods and visit the apartment.

The transplant surgeon was pleased. He was also impressed with Robin. She was just five years old. Yet, she was able to identify each of her medications and knew the correct dosages. He felt left-handed people were definitely more intelligent. Since Robin was a lefty, he was convinced: her ability added credibility to this theory.

In the next week, she was released from the hospital. Grandma and Grandad returned home, taking Ryan with them for a visit. Kay and Robin stayed at the apartment for another month. Both were responding so well they were anxious to get home. It was a special joy and blessing for us to witness this answer to our prayers and the prayers of so many others praying with us. Robin was indeed free from the kidney machine. We gave God the glory and honor with our thanks.

"In all these things we are more than conquerors through him who loved us" (Romans 8:37).

I returned home in time to start the spring ranch work and also to have everything in readiness for the family's homecoming.

"Life is but a Weaving"
My life is but a weaving
Between my Lord and me.
I cannot choose the colors
He worketh steadily.
Oft' times He weaveth sorrow;
And I in foolish pride
Forget He sees the upper
And I the underside.
Not 'til the loom is silent
And the shuttles cease to fly

47

Shall God unroll the canvas
And reveal the reason why.
The dark threads are as needful
In the Weaver's skillful hand
As the threads of gold and silver
In the pattern He has planned.[2]

By Easter, the family was home. We celebrated the miracle of Christ's resurrection. God's love for us was provided when He sacrificed His only Son. After the first man's sin, God had required an animal blood sacrifice from each person annually for the forgiveness of the sin. Christ's shed blood fulfilled God's requirement once and for all for a blood sacrifice as the payment for our sin debt. Then, as God had promised, which had been recorded by the Old Testament prophets, three days later, Christ arose from the dead. He revealed Himself to His followers for a brief time, after which He bodily returned to heaven. When we accept Christ as our Savior, by faith, God brings us back from our spiritually dead condition. Only through Christ's shed blood can we be made acceptable to God. Without being made right, we will spend eternity without Christ, in darkness, separated from God.

They will be punished with everlasting destruction and shut out from the presence of the Lord and from the majesty of his power on the day he comes to be glorified in his holy people and to be marveled at among all those who have believed.

2 Thessalonians 1:9–10

As we witnessed Robin's new physical life, we were better able to understand and appreciate the meaning of "new life in Christ." Just as Robin's body needed to accept the transplant to again be physically complete, we must accept God's Son personally into our lives to be made spiritually complete. In the same manner as Kay and I had to decide to trust and accept, by faith, the surgeon's ability to make Robin physically whole, each of us must also accept, by faith, that Christ's shed blood will make us spiritually whole.

Robin was a new kid at our house. Going on dialysis so young, she hardly remembered having ever felt good. Circumstances would never be the same again. She seemed almost driven to experience and excel at everything. Even at this early age, she revealed her love for people. This was evident in her willingness to share and help others whenever she could. Also, she accepted authority and was always a very obedient child. Her greatest aspiration was to be a doctor or nurse.

At first, Kay and I were overly protective. The drugs Robin took were to suppress the natural immune system the body uses to fight off disease. Anything foreign to the body will naturally put this system on alert. It begins to isolate or reject the intruder to protect the body. In the case of transplanted tissue, it is necessary to disarm this key fighting unit until the new organ is accepted.

The task of the medical team is to maintain a delicate balance between rejecting and accepting without putting too great a risk on the body. Initially, any attack by an infection or disease could complicate success. We did not want Robin to get anything that would upset this balance, jeopardizing the chances of her body continuing to accept the new kidney. Additionally, the transplanted organ was grafted to the inside front wall of the abdomen, where it could be damaged by an external blow.

One notable admonition from the doctor was she should never ride a horse, not even Clip Clop; the saddle horn could damage her kidney. Naturally, we felt it was necessary to shelter her from as many potentially hazardous situations as possible.

Robin was back in preschool, and it did not take her long to catch up with the other children. With Ryan also going, Kay was busy changing roles from "nurse" to "chauffeur." It was a daily thirty-mile round trip. Each day, when the kids were back home, Robin would get them organized. They would divide the rest of their day between playing school and hospital. At one time, we had teddy bears and dolls and their cat "tiger" bandaged up, recovering from sundry accidents and diseases, learning their three R's.

For the spring nursery school program, they chose to reenact the fairy tale, the Seven Dwarfs. Good-natured Ryan was picked to play the dwarf Happy, while Robin was cast for the role of Snow White. She had become somewhat of a celebrity with all the publicity, but more importantly, she was not bashful in front of people. She enjoyed performing.

Robin knew all about fairy tales from her storybooks at the hospital. She had also had a personal encounter with one. After being released from the hospital, during the month she and Kay stayed in Seattle, friends living on Vashon Island invited them to spend a day visiting.

There was only one way to get across to the island. Well, when Robin heard they were going to ride on a ferry, she got excited and asked Kay, "Will the 'fairy' have a blue dress, golden hair, and a magic wand?"

A week before the program was to be presented, we were shocked to discover Robin had chicken pox. This childhood disease is a virus and potentially very risky for a newly transplanted child. Viruses sometimes filter out in the kidney and can cause failure, even under normal conditions. We talked the situation over with her doctor. The resulting decision was to put her in isolation back at the hospital in Seattle. This would

protect her from getting anything else that could further complicate the hopes for a speedy recovery. Additionally, they could
more closely monitor possible signs of rejection. Wow, one day,
we were praising God for the miracle of the transplant, and
the next day, we find ourselves back at the hospital in a state of
worry, stewing over her condition!

God needed to remind us again of the importance of trusting Him. You would have thought the lessons learned during
the years on dialysis and the miracle of the transplant would
have taught us to be strong and trust God for the outcome in
this crisis. They did not! As humans, we are not strong. Even
though we are children of God through salvation, we still have,
within us, the old nature we inherited from the first man. It
keeps telling us we can make it on our own, we do not need
God. When we let this happen, concern over a situation or
thing becomes so strong it soon begins to adversely affect our
lives. The concern becomes a worry, which, in turn, can lead to
frustration and depression.

> I know that nothing good lives in me, that is, in my
> sinful nature. For I have the desire to do what is good,
> but I cannot carry it out. For what I do is not the good
> I want to do; no, the evil I do not want to do—this I
> keep on doing.
>
> Romans 7:18–19

God is still there, wanting to help. He cannot do it if our
backs are turned toward Him while we try to piece things together on our own. By turning around, putting our faith back

in Him, we indicate our need for help. When we are willing to do this, God then replaces our worry or frustration or depression with His peace, both in our hearts and minds. We can then work through the situation or problem, being confident that with His help, we can accept the outcome.

"Trust in the Lord and do good; dwell in the land and enjoy safe pasture. Delight yourself in the Lord, and he will give you the desires of your heart" (Psalm 37:3–4).

We relearned this lesson as Robin recovered from the chicken pox. It became easier for us to trust God in taking care of her rather than to try to protect her from every little thing ourselves.

Kay was more disappointed than Robin about missing the program. Ryan did a great job playing himself, Happy. Robin wanted to be there but seemed to understand and accept the situation.

Shortly after returning from Seattle, it was time for Ryan's fourth birthday. Grandma and Grandad Petrik came to help celebrate. While they were visiting, we took a day off to enjoy some of God's special handiwork. About one hundred miles to the east of where we ranched, the mountains rise majestically. We rode the tram up Mount Howard in the far northeast corner of Oregon. On a cloudless day, you can see miles in every direction. Also, in several states. You almost feel like you are standing on top of the world as you view a small part of God's creation.

Later in the summer, we took our first real vacation in several years. The family decided the place to go was the Washington coast. We really enjoyed being "beach burns." Robin and

Ryan spent hours playing in the sand and surf, experiencing the natural beauty and impressive power of the sea. The sheer joy of seeing two healthy children delighting in another part of God's creation was refreshing to our souls. I even caught a couple of delicious salmon.

When September arrived, Robin was ready for school to start. In our rural community, the kindergarten met each morning in the back half of the cafeteria. This was about ten miles away in the small town of Echo. Robin would get on the bus early each morning and return around noon. All the children adjusted very nicely to each other and loved their teacher. Robin relished the projects and learning. However, it was tough on Kay to see her little girl going away each morning.

In the Pendleton area, the opening of school each fall signals the arrival of a special, exciting event. It is always held during the second week of September. In the early days of the West, one of the big events each fall was a cattle roundup. Cows were turned out on the range in early spring and brought in before winter. Usually, when getting ready for this annual event, the cowboys would have a wild time determining who was best at riding wild horses and roping steers. They were competing with each other in activities that were necessary skills used on the job. These early-day contests between local hands were a forerunners' ritual. Today, it has become the world-famous Pendleton Roundup, one of the premier rodeos in the nation. It is unique in several aspects: it is still entirely a community affair; there are no paid directors, and it is the only major rodeo still held on grass. Every other fall, for years, it has been televised and featured on national programming.

This four-day show also hosts one of the largest gatherings of Native American Indians. Held in conjunction with the rodeo is a nightly Happy Canyon pageant, an outdoor theater production depicting the settlement of this area. The last scene is an early-day frontier-town dance hall featuring a current big name, a country Western star. Everyone at the performance is invited to join in for the rest of the evening.

If you live in the Pendleton area, there is a good chance each year, during the roundup week, you will be enjoying company. This year we were visited by another transplant patient and his wife. He had been transplanted while Robin and Kay were staying in Seattle. They were a nice young couple. We shared our common experiences while taking in many of the festivities associated with this fun week.

We were beginning to feel more like a regular family. The added pressure we had been saddled with for the past few years was finally gone. We could turn our energies toward other activities. Robin was growing fast, catching up on her growth from the years on dialysis. While Ryan had almost caught up with her, she continued holding her own, managing to keep slightly ahead.

The farmland to the west of us was being developed with irrigation. Kay and I made the decision to start developing our place. In October, we dug the first deep-water well. It was a dry area with only an eight-to-ten-inch average annual rainfall. The thought of having enough water to raise better crops was encouraging.

About the same time, Kay started having spells of sickness. We had been assured there would be little likelihood of problems and that it is possible to live a normal life on one kidney. However, we were suspicious when the sickness continued. We scheduled an appointment for her to see a doctor.

He confirmed our apprehension: Kay was pregnant. According to his calculations, we could expect a new baby in early March. This was definitely not classified as a planned event. Especially so soon after she had given up one kidney. We had always felt that two children were the perfect-size family. We soon realized this had been wrong, and it did not take long for us to start feeling the excitement of the anticipated event. Besides, what could be more perfect than to have a child born the very same year as our country's bicentennial?

We felt, since Robin's birthday and Christmas were so close together, it would be nice to make a change. Our decision was to move her birthday celebration to January 22. This was the anniversary date of her kidney transplant. This would become her rebirthday. It would not only serve to separate the two events, Christmas and birthday, but a better way to celebrate the miracle of the transplant. Indeed, she had been given a new life!

Both sets of grandparents came for Christmas. It was an especially meaningful holiday; the kids were so excited. In many ways, it was almost like Robin was having Christmas for the first time. Physically, she was in excellent condition and feeling better than she could remember in her short life. We truly could relate to the often-repeated phrase "Peace on Earth" as we gathered around the tree, exchanging gifts.

The rebirthday party was a big hit. Robin had her very own birthday cake to share with her classmates. While most of the children did not really understand, I feel Robin was beginning to realize the significance of this God-sent miracle. She asked lots of questions about the time on dialysis and expressed genuine thankfulness for not having to use the machine any longer.

We almost had our third child at home. When the appointed time arrived, I drove Kay to the hospital. Rodger Doyle, a bouncing baby boy, arrived within minutes.

Rodger
God's Warrior

"Learn to do good; seek justice, correct oppression; defend the fatherless, plead for the widow" (Isaiah 1:17, RSV).

The pregnancy had gone very smoothly despite the fact Kay only had one kidney. There had been nothing unusual or different from the other births. The doctors had been accurate when they told us we really do not need two kidneys to live a normal life. Kay and the new baby were out of the hospital and home in just a few days. They were greeted by two wide-eyed, excited older siblings.

We hear about kids being spoiled. This new baby did not lack any attention. Neither older sister nor brother could keep their hands off him. He was mothered and always brothered and fit right into the family. Robin had hoped for a baby sister but decided babies were fun no matter which kind.

A great many activities were going on in celebration of the bicentennial. We discovered, after moving to the ranch, the old Oregon Trail had gone right by our place. It was used in the 1800s as a route for the pioneers who came west. It was exciting to think they had traveled so close by.

One of the planned events was for a wagon train to retrace this trail, from west to east, and other routes arriving in Washington, DC, late in 1976. The western portion would follow the Oregon Trail. We had read the complete set of Little House on the Prairie books by Laura Ingalls Wilder to Robin and Ryan. They were excited, anticipating this reenactment of pioneer days.

Robin particularly enjoyed the stories about life in the early days. Living on the ranch in the wide-open spaces allowed her to almost relive most of the pages from those books. They spent hours pretending they were Ma and Pa. They would load up Ryan's wagon with extra clothes and "grub," and pretending Rodger was little Grace, they were off to the banks of Plum Creek. The wagon train was scheduled for an overnight stop in our small town of Echo.

The night it arrived and the next day, we were able to experience history coming alive right before our eyes. There was street dancing and campfires. People from all around the surrounding area came to join in the excitement. The next morning, we saw a real wagon train as it slowly made its way across the prairie. They stopped at our mailbox and let the kids sit up on one of the wagons—a most exciting example of actual travel out of the past and also a dramatic object lesson of the changes and progress that have occurred in a short span of history.

During the summer, we were visited by the kids' great-grandmother, Mom Hull (my grandmother). She was ninety-five and had traveled through this country in a wagon. Pop Hull had been quite a traveler for those days. They had moved several times. In the early 1900s, they had spent time in the mountains east of us, where Pop did some logging. They were en route from California to make a homestead claim in Eastern Montana.

Uncle Gerald, a bachelor, with Aunt Jeanie, a widow, and Mom were traveling around the west, recalling some of the family's early-day movements. Their modern-day travel trailer provided a vivid contrast to the wagons of yesterday. We picnicked with them near an area where they had crossed the Snake River sixty years earlier. The area is now under water from dams constructed along the river. Other changes were evident to them, too. Robin and Ryan enjoyed listening to them reminisce.

The year before, the family had very much enjoyed the coast. We decided it would be fun to go again. Before school started, we made a quick trip to the beach for a few days of relaxation. Robin and Ryan enjoyed playing in the water and collecting all sorts of interesting things. I went out fishing and did catch some salmon. The kids were extremely disappointed they could not go out on the fishing boat with me, but charter-company rules do not allow children under twelve.

A very traumatic experience for mothers is to see their babies going off for the first day of school. Kay had somehow managed the year before with Robin in kindergarten. Since it was for only half a day, it had not seemed too bad. This year would be different! Both Robin and Ryan had to get on the bus by seven o'clock. Robin was not home again until four o'clock. Ryan returned at lunchtime.

It was amazing how fast our kids grew up. While we both thought it was a grand adventure, poor Kay was sure they would never return. And I suppose in a lot of ways, mothers are right.

Once our children start school, they leave the close family nest. We will never again have their total undivided attention.

The brief period before they start school is important. These are critical years for our children as we shepherd them, gradually exposing them to life and the real world. It is felt much of their basic character is molded during this time. We have the responsibility of getting them started off correctly.

Their Christian upbringing is also an invaluable part of this growing-up period. Attending Sunday school and church has always been important to us. The kids enjoyed these activities. Our church in Pendleton was faithful in teaching God's Word. We were all growing in our spiritual lives.

First grade is a fun time for young children as they make the transition from activities to learning. Robin was very anxious to learn. We will never forget the first day when she got off the bus and came running into the house. She was terribly upset and disappointed: she had not learned to read in one day!

Ryan was adjusting well to kindergarten, although he enjoyed the playtime more than the planned activities. It did not take long for everyone to settle down. These early experiences in a small-country school provided an excellent introduction to education. Kay even found it enjoyable to have half a day free to spend with baby Rodger.

Once again, we had an opportunity to share our home. We were asked to host another foreign student attending Portland State University. Ours was married and from Iran. We really enjoyed having Mostafa and Nazy in our home. Robin was very fascinated with the idea of someone from a different land staying with us.

They enjoyed the children. Nazy was expecting and spoke truly little English. Because of Robin's loving way, verbal communication did not seem too important. She would sit or stand remarkably close to Nazy, touching her or holding her hand, attending to whatever she felt was wanted or needed. Mostafa spoke exceptionally good English. It was interesting to visit with him about the vast differences between our cultures and religions.

We had occasion to visit them in Portland after their baby was born. Also, we corresponded with them until they returned to Iran shortly before our two countries broke off relations. Our family has often wondered how they were doing since the baby would have American citizenship.

We spent Thanksgiving at Grandma and Grandpa Nelson. It was a delightful day with all the relatives, including Great-Grandma and Grandpa Barnes (Grandma Nelson's parents). The next day we visited Kay's and my old college roommates (our best friends had also married) who farmed in Southern Oregon. Roger and Donna have two boys. One was the same age as Robin, the other a little younger than Ryan. We had not visited with them for some time. We enjoyed sharing with each other and catching up on the past few years.

Near to where they live is an interesting tourist attraction. It is called Wildlife Safari. You actually drive through the park and observe animals in a natural setting. The kids enjoyed this adventure. They became very hyper whenever a wild beast ventured too close, but of course, this added to the drama!

There was another reason we had insisted on Grandma inviting us for Thanksgiving. Elvis Presley was giving a concert at the University of Oregon. He had been the king of rock and roll during our high school and college days. Kay and I thought it would be fun to see him perform live. We had a wonderful time reminiscing. Both of us had enjoyed our college days.

What a wonderful Christmas our family enjoyed in 1976! Little Rodger was into everything on and under the tree. Robin and Ryan were excited about helping their brother get into the spirit of the season. Both sets of grandparents were with us.

We paused to reflect on the past year and again celebrate the gift of God's Son to us. We found we had much to be thankful for.

As Americans, we are truly blessed. Freedom is one thing we often take for granted. It is wonderful to have the freedom to worship and praise God, each in our own way. This and the many financial and medical blessings we have been privileged to enjoy are truly gifts from God.

Our kids were in Christmas programs of both Sunday school and regular school. Kay and I were delighted with their performances. Robin thoroughly loved reciting her parts. She never missed a line.

Kay and I had intended to continue celebrating Robin's birthday on the rebirthday date. We thought it had worked very well. This year, we found out our idea had been all right, but why not have two celebrations? I do not recall exactly; however, I believe the grandmas were on Robin's side. Anyhow, when her birthday, Christmas Eve, arrived, we ended up having a party. From then on, we have commemorated both her birthday and rebirthday.

Robin was rapidly changing. She had not stopped growing since the transplant. The doctor had gradually reduced the large dosage of immunosuppression medication. Her body was accepting the new kidney without any problem. It worked flawlessly. By this time, the amounts of Imuran and prednisone were minimal. The round puffy face, a characteristic side effect of those drugs, had disappeared.

Robin expressed an interest in playing the piano. Since we had the one Kay had used, she inquired and found a good piano teacher who would teach young children. Robin started lessons about a month after beginning first grade. Practicing became another favorite pastime. She enjoyed learning the necessary skills.

One of the highlights in children's lives is having a best friend. Sometimes we meet a certain special person, and from the very first we know our friendship will last forever. This happened with Robin and Julie Potts early in first grade. Having both grown up in Christian families gave them common ground. However, more than this was their immediate trust and sharing with each other. Robin was the organizer while Julie provided the spunk. From then on, it was pals and friends through thick and thin.

In the spring, Robin had her first piano audition. She had learned the piano pieces very well. At the piano recital, her teacher was incredibly pleased not only to give her the usual certificate but to award her a gold pin. This was a recognition of the highest honors for her adjudication, sponsored by the National Guild of Piano Teachers. She was becoming a very accomplished musician in addition to being tops in her first-grade class.

On Valentine's Day, they all exchanged little cards. Robin enjoyed making sure each was exactly right. Others in the class had done the same. To Robin's surprise, one of her classmates had a really serious crush on her. He brought her a large heart-shaped box of candy!

The new kidney was functioning very well. The doctors put Robin on a once-a-year schedule for checkups. Sometime around the first of each year, we would go over to visit for an evaluation of the blood work and other tests. We would also make a point of visiting Dr. Hickman. He was her favorite doctor. Also, he continued to use information concerning her at medical conferences. She was an outstanding example of successful peritoneal dialysis.

It seemed like we had been continually on the go during the first year after Robin's transplant. Now our lives were taking on the aspects of a more normal family. These activities centered around school and church. The children were getting more involved.

On the ranch, we were continuing with the irrigation development. The project was nearing completion, and we were giving thoughtful consideration to selling the property. We wanted to get back into a dry-land farming operation.

Beginning second grade, Robin experienced one of the great disappointments many children endure. Her best friend, Julie, was moving. The Pott family was going back to Spokane. Even though they made a pact to stay connected and write often, this reassurance did not lessen the sadness of such an important loss. While Robin found it easy to make friends and adjust to changing circumstances, she would never have a more perfect relationship.

The next few years were filled with happy and exciting times. The kids were growing, and each began to take on their own individuality. Robin continued to excel at her schoolwork and music. She was fascinated with books and enjoyed reading a wide range of stories. She was rereading all the Laura Ingalls Wilder books. Bible stories were also a favorite.

The children were anxious to travel. They enjoyed going places, even if it was just a family picnic in the mountains or to the river for a swim. For Thanksgiving, we decided to make a trip to Minnesota. Grandma and Grandad Petrik wanted us to have the traditional turkey dinner at their house. My sister and her family also lived in the same town. We would all be together for the holiday. Our kids were elated at the thought of flying in a big jet and looked forward to playing in the snow with their cousins.

The best scheduling for a nonstop flight was to leave from Spokane. It would be an early morning departure. You could almost see the wheels turning in Robin's mind as she helped us work out the details. Her hopes, of course, were to visit Julie. Since it was a 200-mile drive, we decided it would be best to go up the day before and stay overnight. Upon checking into the motel, Robin was bugging her mom to call the Potts if she could visit Julie. They invited us for dessert. We had a good visit, especially the girls.

It was an excellent flight. Everyone enjoyed this new experience. Kay and I had flown before, however, never with three kids. They wanted to know everything about anything having to do with flying. When they were not trying to see out one of the windows, they were pretending to be a pilot or stewardess. Robin was really fascinated by it all. She wanted to know if we would fly when we died and went to heaven. We tried to help her understand that, yes, we would fly, but no, we would not need an airplane.

She was learning music composition along with piano skills. We were surprised and pleased when she wrote a song, "Bad Guys Comin'." Mrs. Conway, her teacher, submitted it for the national competition. She received a bronze pin; this was quite an accomplishment for a seven-year-old. Also, a silver pin for her adjudication. Both programs were sponsored by the National Guild of Piano Teachers.

By this time, Robin was having real difficulty trying to decide on a career. She wanted to be a nurse, a teacher, an airline stewardess, and a mother. We were quick to assure her she did not need to decide yet. There would be time to make the right choice soon enough.

The kids looked forward each year to daily vacation Bible school. It would have been all right with Robin to have gone to school all year long. She enjoyed any kind of school, Sunday school, Bible school, or regular school. That year, Robin not only went to the vacation Bible school at our church but talked Kay into letting her go to a second session at another church.

She enjoyed being challenged. The Bible was coming alive to her. She wanted to know everything about God and His Word. Our Christian education committee decided to make the summer Bible school special in a city park. They invited the Friends

Puppets from Vancouver, Washington. They have an incredibly special ministry with kids.

What excitement to watch and listen to these funny little creatures! They made Bible truths fun to learn. It was, indeed, a refreshing change from the normal type of more structured activities. Both Robin and Ryan responded to God's calling. They committed their lives to Christ because of this ministry.

At various times, in our family discussions, we had talked about the importance of having the right relationship with God. Also, in Sunday school, the kids were continually learning about this from God's Word. Up until that moment, they had not come to the point of realizing they had a personal need for salvation. This was truly a highlight for them as they marveled at this gift God offers through His Son, the Lord Jesus Christ.

We were overwhelmed unexpectedly on a day when we received a letter from an attorney. It concerned a lady we never met. This teacher had faithfully followed Robin's progress since hearing about her during the fund drive. Every holiday, she would remember her favorite little girl with either a card or a small gift. She had passed away. Reading on, the attorney was advising us she had left Robin her savings account. Once again, we sensed a feeling of God's love expressed through people.

Robin loved surprises. One day, Kay received a telephone call from Spokane. Julie's folks were coming to Stanfield for their high-school reunion. Her mom wanted to know if it would be all right for Julie to spend the night. Neither of the girls could have been happier. Robin spent the next several days making plans for the visit. She detailed out every activity for them and just could not wait. They had a super time except for one thing: it was over too soon.

By the time she had completed third grade, her state tests had indicated she was at a tenth-grade reading-skill level. There was thought given at this point to advancing her a grade if she continued developing so rapidly. However, Kay and I felt if this were to happen, it should be put off until more of the basic work in all different areas had been completed, especially math.

Both Robin and Ryan expressed an interest in being baptized. Baptism symbolizes union with Christ. It pictures Jesus's death, burial, and resurrection and is required by Christ after our confession of faith. Because of His sacrifice, through faith, we are raised from spiritual death into new life.

"And this water symbolizes baptism that now saves you also—not the removal of dirt [...] towards God. It saves you by the resurrection of Jesus Christ" (1 Peter 3:21).

They chose Father's Day to make this public confession of this faith. Not only honoring their heavenly Father through this step of obedience but bringing joy to my heart, their earthly father.

We had gotten a camper for our pickup. All of us enjoyed exploring interesting and scenic areas around the Northwest. One interesting weekend trip was to view Hells Canyon, the nation's deepest gorge. The Snake River runs through it and is the topographic boundary between Oregon and Idaho. It is in a very desolate and remote area. Getting up to the top after crossing from Oregon into Idaho required trying to navigate a single gravel road cut out of the canyon wall.

We decided to stay at the bottom and view this natural wonder the following day. The kids were horrified upon reading a large sign at the entrance to the camping site. This area is noted for its natural state, which includes an abundance of rattlesnakes. The sign was a specific warning to beware and be cautious of these unpredictable creatures. We did not have much trouble with kids wandering away from camp. They imagined every rock or stick they encountered either was a snake or had one under it.

The view is spectacular from the top. It is humbling to realize the greatness of God revealed through this vast creation. When we understand God knows everything happening here on the earth and even the inmost thoughts of our hearts and minds, we are in awe. We give Him the praise and honor He deserves. To do this is to do God's will.

Viewing this natural wonder, we could relate our dependence on God and His provision and care for us over the past few difficult years to something Jesus had talked about.

Consider how the lilies grow. They do not labor or spin. Yet I tell you, not even Solomon in all his splendor was dressed like one of these. If that is how God clothes the grass of the field, which is here today and tomorrow thrown into the fire, how much more will he clothe you, O you of little faith! And do not set your heart on what you will eat or drink; do not worry about it. For the pagan world runs after all such things, and your Father knows that you need them.

But seek his kingdom, and these things will be given
to you as well.

Luke 12:27–31

There is nothing concealed [...] that will not be made
known [...] Are not two sparrows sold for a penny? Yet
not one of them will fall to the ground apart from the
will of your Father. And even the very hairs of your
head are numbered. So don't be afraid; you are worth
more than sparrows.

Matthew 10:26–31

By the spring of 1979, the irrigation development was complete. We had deepened the original well and drilled a second
one. All the buried mainline and circles were in place. The system was operational.

We raised a variety of crops, keeping us busy all summer.
One of the different things we tried was growing carrots for
a cannery. In addition, we had several acres of other vegeta-
bles for field trials. We grew beans, cucumbers, and sweet corn
along with some melons. After the fieldman finished taking his
samples, we were left with a large amount of produce. We decided to market our share on a U-Pick basis. Robin and Ryan
enjoyed helping weigh the produce and counting out change
for people.

By late fall, we were seriously looking toward selling the
property. As the negotiations began to come together, Kay and
I decided to surprise the family for Christmas. We would take
them to Disneyland. We had recently bought a new pickup.

This would be a good excuse to try it out. Using the camper to travel in, we could enjoy many of the sites en route. We spent Christmas day with Grandma and Grandpa Nelson in Springfield, leaving there on the twenty-sixth for our big adventure in California.

During this trip, we discovered Robin's knack for recording her experiences. In this way, she could relive them later without missing any important details. She had received a cassette recorder for her birthday. Supplied with extra tapes, she very diligently made a daily record of our travels.

Some of her commentaries included how she felt about various aspects of the trip. Naturally, the kids were very anxious to be at Disneyland; however, we had agreed to take in some of the attractions along the way. Our plan was to drive straight home nonstop on the return trip. En route, they became frustrated at times when we made an occasional unscheduled detour.

For instance, her records reveal she definitely felt if you had seen one redwood tree, you did not need to take the time to see another, even if it might be slightly different from the last one. My emphasis in college had been in botany, so I was interested in seeing the biggest, oldest, and so on. She and the boys were quite impatient to keep moving. We managed to make the necessary compromises and were able to keep on schedule despite some murmurings.

Taking in Disneyland, Knott's Berry Farm, MarineLand, and Universal Studios, I am sure we did not miss very many rides or events. We even had the good fortune to get front-row seats for a Pat Boone concert. He was a refreshing change from rushing not to miss out on anything.

The highlight of our visit was the Disneyland New Year's Eve celebration. What a grand show complete with fireworks! It made quite an impression on these ranchers from Oregon. There really is a lot of sparkle and excitement associated with Southern California.

We celebrated Kay's birthday on January 3, before leaving for home. Our plans called for one more stop. We wanted to visit the Roy Rogers museum at Victorville. We were glad we had made this detour, for it was an enjoyable place to visit.

As we talked about the excitement and glamour of this Christmas holiday, we could not help but recall the events surrounding Christ's birth 1,900 plus years ago. Those lowly shepherds must have been excited witnessing heaven open and herald angels proclaim Christ's birth. We also marveled at how many seemingly miss the true spirit of Christmas.

5

Moving

After safely returning, we finished the details concerning the sale. We set the closing date, but since the sale would be completed before the school year was over, we retained possession of the house. This would give us time until the first of June to relocate. It proved to be a good decision as it took longer than we had anticipated to find a new ranch. We felt, since so many changes had taken place with the treatment of kidney disease, it would be wise to move into the state of Washington. We would feel more comfortable continuing with Robin's medical history there. Our prayer was for God to lead us to just the right place.

We were amazed, as were Robin's teachers, at how she would tackle each new challenge. It did not matter whether it was a study assignment or an activity she created for herself. She had a special gift for becoming totally committed to the task at hand. Each would receive 110 percent effort until it was completed.

The Department of Education sponsored a program to familiarize elementary-age students with writing skills. Robin was chosen to attend this seminar. An author would evaluate their writings and help encourage and motivate them in these skills. It would be held at Blue Mountain Community College, which is in Pendleton.

Ahead of time, each participant was asked to originate several make-believe characters and write a series of short stories about them. Robin created Hermy Truckers, his family, and friends. She wrote seven imaginative tales. At the conclusion of the appointed day, all the children's stories were bound together in one folder and given to the college library. This was a nice honor for these young people.

I was busy trying to find a suitable place for us. This required spending much of my time with realtors, looking at their offerings. By May, we had located what we felt was an excellent property. Our realtor scheduled a meeting with the attorneys to complete the closing. We were to meet with them in Pullman, Washington, on May 17 (our wedding anniversary).

Everyone was there on schedule. However, during the afternoon, the other parties involved decided not to sell. While we were somewhat discouraged, we had considered other places, so we would not be starting over from scratch. The next day, Sunday, May 18, we had a leisurely brunch in Colfax and headed out to look at other properties in the area.

It seemed to be getting dark outside for midday. We assumed a big thunderstorm was approaching from the west and wondered if it would be a gully washer. By this time, it was so dark we had to turn the car lights on. In the headlights, it looked like it was beginning to snow. We were really puzzled, as it did not appear quite right. Farmers working in the fields around us had also turned on their tractor lights. It was a few

minutes past one o'clock in the afternoon. As darkness completely enveloped us, we began to have a very eerie feeling.

We turned on the radio. To our amazement, the airwaves
were full of confusing chatter about the eruption of Mount St.
Helens. We were some three hundred miles directly east of the
big blast. As we turned back to take refuge in Colfax, we were
totally bewildered by the spectacular occurrence taking place
before our eyes. What an awesome display of power! A mountain was destroyed, and tiny pieces of it, the ash, were falling
out of the sky around us.

We made it back to Colfax and were able to get a motel
room, the last one available. The state police closed all high-
ways. Those travelers stranded after us were put up and made
comfortable in schools and churches.

The situation was one of perplexity. We were amazed at the
conflicting reports being broadcast about what to do. There
had been no forewarning that the eruption would be of this
magnitude. Additionally, it happened on a Sunday, and most
government offices were closed. Not one authority or agency
seemed to know how to manage the questions and problems.

At first, Robin wondered if this might be a sign of the
world ending. We did not feel it was. Earthquakes and
eruptions occur from time to time in various places
around the globe. We talked some about what Jesus
had told His disciples when they asked Him about
the end times. When you hear of wars and rumors of
wars, do not be alarmed. Such things must happen,
but the end is still to come. Nation will rise against

nation, and kingdom against kingdom. There will be
earthquakes in various places, and famines. [...]
No one knows about the day or hour, not even the angels in heaven, not the Son, but only the Father.

Mark 13:7–8, 32

The cloud had passed by the next morning. The sun was
shining very brightly over the most desolate-looking landscape you can imagine. There had not been any wind. The trees
and buildings, everything was colored gray. There was about
a three-inch accumulation on the ground. The ash would fluff
out of the way when you walked through it. It was very heavy,
and your footprints had an exaggerated appearance. The whole
scene looked like a moonscape.

Travel was not recommended. From the radio and television
reports, we surmised that Colfax was about sixty highway miles
from the southern edge of the path the cloud had taken. We
were anxious to get back home. Early in the morning, we ventured out on our own. Using handkerchiefs, we made masks
for the kids and ourselves. Then, asking the Lord for traveling
mercies, we left the temporary security of our motel room for
the uncertainty of the highway.

It was a quiet ride. The passing countryside had the appearance of how we imagined the aftermath of a holocaust might
look. Animals were just standing in the fields, not knowing
what to do. Cars and trucks were abandoned in ditches, left
where they had veered off the road during the ash storm. Farm-
steads looked as if they had been vacated. Nothing was moving,
and everything was a light gray color.

When we finally got out of the ash area and took off our homemade masks, we looked like ghosts. The outside and inside of the car and our clothes were coated with the fine particles. They seemed magnetic, sticking to everything. The filtering system for the car's engine and air conditioning unit was completely plugged. Having stopped at the first town we came to for a new air filter and to do some cleaning, we were then able to continue. We never completely got all the ash out of that car.

After we were back on the road, relieved we had not suffered any apparent damage, we were thankful the sellers had changed their minds. It was some time before anyone knew for certain what the consequences would be. One thing we could be sure of: the cleanup would be a gigantic task. We were thankful to get back home.

As a family, we approached the sale of our farm and the pending move as an adventure. While we realized a new area would have many uncertainties, we were also looking forward to new challenges. We enjoyed our friends and living in the Pendleton area; however, it was time to move on. Kay and I had relocated several times over the years. We had always enjoyed making changes. The kids loved to have us show them pictures and talk about other areas we had lived or visited. They each had active imaginations and were never tired of asking "what if" questions: "What if nobody likes us?" "What if we do not like the new school?" "What if we cannot find a place to move?" What if? What if?

We had looked at a farm north of Spokane earlier in the year. As it turned out, this area had received only a light dusting of ash. The owners were willing to sell. Unbelievably, we were able to make the necessary arrangements to take possession and complete the move by the fifteenth of June.

The city of Deer Park is in a beautiful area surrounded by mountains. It is not far from the "big" city of Spokane and is large by comparison with the smaller towns we were used to in Eastern Oregon. It is an excellent area in which to raise children and close to many good recreational spots. It was purported to have excellent schools. We made the transition without fanfare and were pleased with our relocation.

6

The Yellow Brick Road

Robin and Ryan were amazed when they discovered the size of the new school. There were as many kids in each grade as had been in the entire student body, K–12, back in Oregon. Needless to say, they were anxious to check this out. However, after they were registered and had looked over the facilities, they decided it was going to be all right. Rodger was not in school yet, so he would not know the difference.

Another exciting discovery was the community swimming pool. This by itself just might be worth making the move! Within a week, both older children were enjoying swimming lessons—a terrific opportunity to make new friends and meet classmates.

The most exciting thing about moving to the Spokane area for Robin was living near her best friend, Julie. Now they were close enough so they could spend lots of time together. They would have preferred it if they had gone to the same church and school, but just being within twenty miles of each other was a dream come true. Much to their delight, Ken, Julie's older brother, got a job with me, which gave them additional opportunities to hitch back and forth.

The kids adjusted to the new school without many problems. They were glad we had been adventuresome enough to make a change. As it was a much larger school, there were a number of others as academically advanced a Robin. The challenge of competing motivated her. She continued giving more than 100-percent effort to ensure herself a position at or near the top. To accomplish this and not miss out on anything required good organization of her time. She was starting to develop good study habits.

Another exciting thing about relocating was finding a new church. We spent the summer visiting different congregations, looking for just the right one. We found our church home after trying out eleven or so. Interestingly, we settled on the very first one we had visited. We joined with this group of believers and, before long, were getting involved in various aspects of church life.

One of the activities our new church offered was the Awana program. This is a high-energy club centered around Bible memorization and the stuff of God's Word. The kids enjoyed this, and we were thankful for the scriptural teaching they were getting.

Being further north and at a higher elevation, we were in real-winter country now. With Christmas approaching, we appreciated the changing season. Snow adds a special beauty to the landscape. The pine trees looked like they had been decorated with white frosting—a picture-perfect setting for our holiday celebration. With grateful hearts, we thanked God for

His provisions, both spiritual and material. We could say, without any reservations, He had brought us to this new place.

Kay was a stickler regarding the benefits of good oral hygiene. And of course, taking diligent care of our teeth is an important part of learning responsibility about our bodies. Throughout the dialysis years, we had constantly struggled with maintaining an adequate calcium level in Robin's system. We had done the best job we could; however, she had developed some problems with the formation of her adult teeth. It had been suggested she see a good orthodontist. He started her with braces to help correct this.

Robin enjoyed fifth grade. Her confidence was growing as she successfully made all the necessary adjustments to a new school and community. She was pleased when they asked her to play the piano for her class's singing part in the annual Christmas program. Also, she was learning to play the flute and enjoyed the school band.

With all the activities and schoolwork, plus a lot of additional reading, Robin began having headaches. Our first thought was she was not getting enough rest or possibly was putting too much pressure on herself to keep up with the demands of her schedule.

When they persisted, we scheduled an appointment with an eye doctor. She needed glasses. This can be a trying experience for any young girl. The more we talked about it and discussed the alternatives—continued headaches and the possibility of her eyes getting worse—she decided it could be bearable. Kay and Robin decided the best way to oversee this situation might be to create a totally new look. This really made a hit, and the drudgery of having to start wearing glasses did not seem nearly so objectionable.

She was pleased to learn that she had been voted clubber of the year by the Awana leaders. Each year, one boy and one girl are selected for this honor, based on attitude and achievement over the past nine months. Her extra effort was paying off.

Before the school year ended, Robin was already making plans for the summer. She wanted to go to church camp and continue with swimming lessons. Her hope was to get far enough along with the Red Cross program so she could instruct at the pool in future years. She really enjoyed swimming and would take lessons in the morning, spending the afternoons at the pool, practicing. While she did not possess a lot of natural athletic ability, she was a good student and very willing to make the necessary additional effort to get the needed certificates.

The campgrounds were on Lake Coeur d'Alene, a beautiful area in Idaho. Julie also went, which added to the excitement of their first camping experience. They learned a lot about God and having a good relationship with others in a very natural setting. Besides swimming and canoeing, they went hiking and had an enjoyable time out of doors. Ryan also went.

Upon returning from this fun-filled activity, both were ready to help us plan a camping vacation. We agreed it would be nice, and if possible, later in the summer, we might be able to take a mini vacation in Canada.

Getting acquainted with different areas, you find most communities have certain traditions or festivals, usually a summertime activity. These events recall something from the past as a theme but serve to enhance civic pride. The Deer Park area does this, and each summer, people from the surrounding tricounty area gather for a Settlers Day picnic, complete with a parade through town.

Nineteen eighty-one was a year of added significance. It was the diamond jubilee celebration. Arrangements had been made for a special grand marshal. Kay consented to escort him and the judges to their appointed places. I helped with traffic control and decorations for the viewing stand.

Robin oversaw our entry in the juniors' parade. The kids won second place for their "Young Pioneers Salute to the Settlers" float, which was constructed around our garden tractor and trailer. They managed very well, even though the horse entry following them kept nibbling on the hay and grain they were using for added effect. After the kids' parade had passed, it was time for the main event.

Montie Montana presided over the parade. He really made a "grand" grand marshal. A veteran of many Hollywood movies and a featured trick-rope artist, he was a very fitting choice for this special day.

The Settlers Day president invited us to have dinner with them and Montie Montana that evening. We were amazed at what an outstanding example of humility and genuine concern for people he exemplified. He had performed for countless audiences and heads of state, including the Queen of England. We will always have fond memories of this special day. Robin enjoyed him and had to have his autograph.

For some time, Robin had wanted an outdoor project of her very own. She was very fond of cute, cuddly bunnies, so she decided to start raising rabbits. She could not stand the thought of eating them; however, she enjoyed handling and taking care of them. She started out on a small scale—one doe and one buck—with the idea of having some little bunnies to play with. It does not take long to learn your multiplication tables in a rabbit hutch. With a lot of loving care, she soon was enjoying a bunny boom. While she was not about to sell them for eating, she had to do something, so she started doing some trading. By the time school started in the fall, we had brown, white, black, long-haired, and an assortment of bunnies in all sizes, colors, and shapes.

When school started, Robin settled into the fall routine and activities with gusto. This would be her last year at middle school and the Awana program. In addition to these normal activities, she was singing with the junior choir at church and playing the flute in the sixth-grade band. Learning and school were her favorite pastimes. She was anxious to please her parents and teachers and willingly enjoyed doing those little extra things that make activities special. She wanted every detail to be correct.

Each fall, at Halloween time, the Awana clubbers came out to our farm for hayrides and a wiener roast. All the kids from the little tots and up enjoy getting out for this sort of activity, especially the town kids who seldom have an occasion to enjoy the wide-open spaces. Robin would organize a touch-and-see area with lots of friendly animals for the kids to play with. She would supervise the activities. Her greatest joy seemed to be in helping and seeing to it that everyone had an enjoyable time.

The Little Angels Choir was a big hit. Robin had one of the solo parts, which she thoroughly enjoyed. Each of the singers knew their individual parts well. Mrs. Fecht, their leader, always seemed to get a little extra from them, which really made each performance special. She also directed the high-school choir, and both groups were invited to sing on television. They were guests on a Christian children's program. The thought of being on television was an exciting event to look forward to. They performed admirably.

By her birthday time and Christmas, she had many super friends. She wanted to have a special party. At this preteen age, they enjoy fantasy land. Girls can get excited imagining how things could or should be while anticipating the teenage years.

Trying to envision what it is going to be like when they are really grown up is fun. Kay and Robin decided they would plan her twelfth birthday party around the theme of magic. Kendrix and Co., a fine young magician, agreed to come and put on his show for the girls. What a time they had, watching him perform "magic" right before their eyes! In no time, he had them, so to speak, eating out of his hands.

We enjoyed a blessed Christmas, marveling at how fast our children were growing up. All three were now in school and excited about every activity and learning experience. During vacation, we took in one of the performances of the Ice Capades. We were impressed by the beauty and grace of each skater. Realizing the dedication to training and practice these skaters must maintain is a good example for us of how we should always strive to do our best.

Indeed, God was willing to give us His best, His Son, and we should be willing to give our best at whatever we do to please Him.

Robin had won many awards in the Awana club program for Scripture memorization and understanding of God's Word. Before the year was over, she had completed all the required work. Because of her dedication in the application of this learning in her own life, she won their highest honor. The Timothy Award, a beautiful trophy, is given in recognition of obedience to God in following His admonition to us.

"Study to shew thyself approved unto God, a workman that needeth not to be ashamed" (2 Timothy 2:15, KJV).

Receiving this kind of recognition was a very fitting way to complete the elementary years. The effort and learning necessary to complete each milestone in our lives will serve to help us meet the new challenges we will encounter as we continue our life adventure.

In June, we made what was becoming an annual affair, our summer trip to the ocean. This year, however, we decided to make it a little more special for the family. We rented a charter fishing boat on our own so that everyone could go out deep-sea fishing. Each year previously, only Grandpa and I would get to go out fishing. The kids did not think this was fair at all.

What fun most of us had, as the fishing was fantastic! We were able to catch our limit of fourteen fish in something less than two hours. Ryan and Robin loved it. Robin caught the most, five (hers plus those for the sicklies), and Ryan tied with Grandad for the biggest (twenty-five pounds).

I mentioned most of us had a fun time; unfortunately, Kay and Rodger were seasick from the time we left the dock until the next day. They were not able to enjoy our family adventure with the same joyous recounting until sometime later.

7

Junior High School

Finally, being in junior high was a dream come true. Changing classes, having different teachers and seemingly a lot more activities was one exciting part of growing up, which motivated Robin. Everything would be different this fall. The thought of turning thirteen and becoming a real teenager made this adventure all more exciting. She would even be riding a different school bus than her brothers, going off earlier in the morning and getting home an hour before them. She felt the subject matter and learning would be much more in-depth and stimulating.

Robin was not disappointed when the school year began. She loved changing classes, having a locker, her teachers, and the challenges and made friends with the kids from all the diverse groups normally found in a junior high. Some of these friends became special, but she tried hard not to exclude anyone.

For years by then, we had been studying the Bible and praying together as a family. We had done this on a regular basis. Family devotions is something you must want to do together. We have found one of the best ways is to involve each other as we investigate God's Word.

We had a special time on Thursdays after dinner when we studied a portion of Scripture. Then we had time for giving praise, making announcements, and talking about things we wanted to pray about. It was not only an enjoyable time to learn truths about God and how to apply them to our everyday lives, but it was an excellent opportunity for children to learn how to pray.

Now that Robin had completed the Awana program, she was spending additional time on her own in Bible study and prayer. Often, she would come to us with questions about things she had difficulty understanding or areas she had problems with. We would try to help her discover where those answers could be found in God's Word.

She was a super organizer. Her life was becoming compartmentalized. There were specific times set aside for each different task. She was comfortable with this kind of routine. Bible study and prayer were an important part of her schedule.

A difficult part of the junior high years is handling the many physical and emotional changes occurring almost daily. It is a difficult transition from childhood to young adulthood. Robin seemed to move through his period without an overly amount of trauma. However, she definitely was experiencing feelings of awkwardness with herself and occasionally very intense feelings of low self-esteem and rejection by her peers. This is a difficult part of the growing-up process. For instance, at times, she was very unhappy with her looks. At other times, she did not feel there was a single person who cared anything about her. In many ways, she was able to deal with these normal frustrations through studying and understanding God's Word.

The privileges and responsibilities of a teenager were major concerns to Robin. She continually wanted to talk about these key areas. Each of us comes to the point of wanting to start taking over accountability for our lives. Turning thirteen is about the time this comes into focus. The exact time this process begins and how long it will last can vary considerably. However, this milestone is a perfect opportunity to develop specific guidelines. We were sure the next few years would be critical. Different authorities we had read seemed to agree changes and conflicts are normal teenage behavior. Our sanity was as much at stake as Robin's unless we made some agreement.

Naturally, as parents, we want our children to become responsible, caring, and loving adults. At this age, specifics are extremely important. It was made clear: we were responsible for working out the details by December 24! The last couple of months before her birthday, she reminded us daily. You might say she was beginning to earn the art of nagging. As was her style, she attacked this situation with the usual extra effort.

She was delighted to find a "legal document" in her birthday present (see the Appendix section). Kay and I feel strongly about the importance of accountability. We do not feel rigid rules and regulations are appropriate. We discussed our feelings with Robin and were in full agreement.

As Christian parents, we must, together with our teenagers, trust God and His Word for direction. In this manner, teenagers learn to accept responsibility for their actions and lives more effectively. And in turn, we honor God's Word.

"Fathers, do not exasperate your children; instead, bring them up in training and instruction of the Lord" (Ephesians 6:4).

Our mission is to guide, not dictate. As parents, we need to keep communications open. Fortunately, God accepts us as we are and expects us to do the same with our children as well as others.

December 1982 was the most exciting time ever for Robin. Early in the month, she found out that her braces were finally coming off. The problems with her teeth had been fully corrected. Next, to our surprise, we found she no longer needed glasses. She could not have wished for a more perfect way to enter the teenage years. Kay and I were indeed proud of our young lady. We knew Robin was ready for the added challenges and responsibilities of a rapidly developing young adult.

We paused to celebrate Christmas amidst the pressures and activities of a full life. Robin wanted clothes and some books; the boys wanted no clothes, just toys. We shared our love through the act of exchanging gifts, reminding ourselves once again God's love is sending Jesus, His Son.

We were an early-to-bed, early-to-rise family. Kids were always in bed by nine o'clock. Also, the use of the phone was by asking first.

Several days following Christmas, Robin came up to me and said, "Dad, I've been thinking about the 'document' I got, and I'm going to make a few changes. I'm thirteen now, and I feel I should be able to have a later bedtime than the boys." Getting no argument from me, she continued, "And another thing: I feel I'm old enough to use the phone without asking permission; I will limit calls to ten minutes." Still no argument; she asked, "That should be okay, shouldn't it?" I assured her it was, and she was off to phone one of her friends. These were very reasonable changes—an effective way to start developing her own responsibility.

All three kids were doing well in school. They enjoyed their separate activities. Robin continued to make the high-honor roll and was keeping well ahead with her studies. She was anxious to learn about a new program that her school was selected to institute. The Deer Park junior high was the first to be picked in Eastern Washington for Natural Helpers.

The Natural Helpers program was set up in cooperation with the state system of education. The primary goal was to help counteract the problems of drug and alcohol abuse. An integral part of this program is creating a more open atmosphere among young people from different socioeconomic cliques. By helping each other, they can begin overcoming feelings of low self-worth and insignificance.

Natural Helpers are selected by the kids themselves. They each pick someone they would have confidence in going to for leadership or help. This group would then be available to anyone having problems. Not that they would have any specific answers, but they would be good listeners and help direct others toward getting meaningful counsel. The concept of listening and helping form within is a safe way to broaden communication.

Robin was one of those selected for this key role. The Natural Helpers went on a retreat for several days to develop skills in listening and helping. They learned a great deal about interacting and giving themselves from this unique retreat experience. An interesting and valuable activity associated with meaningful interaction was developing hugging skills. When Robin returned from the retreat, the family learned there were seven or eight different embraces representing various levels of concern and support.

Before long, it became apparent that this young-person-to-young-person interplay is a powerful help in overcoming the loneliness and isolation teenagers feel. As barriers start coming down, there is less temptation to experiment. This kind of atmosphere makes it much easier for young people to say no to behavior considered unacceptable.

Spring is always a welcome season. Suddenly, unexpectedly, the grass greens and flowers burst forth in a dazzling array of color and beauty. In a similar fashion, the long hard hours of study and practice on the piano and musical instruments blossom into a rewarding crescendo of music. Spring concerts, parades, and recitals provide those same kinds of unexpected pleasures.

Music was an added joy for Robin. She thoroughly enjoyed performing. She was playing piano with a stage band. This group included twenty or so of the more accomplished musicians in the junior high. They were the highlight at concerts and athletic events. Also, she played a piano solo at the regional music competition, sang in the church youth choir, and played flute in the marching band.

Love also blossoms at this time of year. Twenty months of May prior to that time, I had lost my heart to Kay. And a total of fifty springs had passed for Grandad and Grandma Petrik. Their golden-wedding anniversary celebration would take place during the Memorial Day weekend, and we all wanted to be with them for this important occasion. Since our schools were not out until mid-June, we felt it would not hurt the kids to miss a few days. Kay and I took turns driving, allowing us to go straight through from Washington to Minnesota.

We arrived in time to help put the finishing touches on the decoration at the reception hall. It was a large gathering of friends and relatives from near and far. The big-party atmosphere Robin loved. She was busy with her cousins, helping where needed while meeting and greeting new people. We all enjoyed the excitement of the festivities.

Vacationing can be fun. Our return plans included doing sightseeing and a little visiting. Our agenda called for stops at Mount Rushmore and Yellowstone National Park. After the final pictures and fond goodbyes were said, we were off.

I believe ranching is in my blood! Our first stop was to visit Aamolds, who live in eastern South Dakota. Larry and I had worked together at the bank in Portland. This had been a long time ago. Since then, both of us had gone into farming and ranching. While he and I looked over their operation, our families were busy getting reacquainted. We enjoyed catching up on the past years and comparing notes on our mutual concerns and aspirations.

We marveled at how easily our children found shared areas of interest. After enjoying the delicious supper Gayle had prepared, we gathered in the living room. Larry lit his pipe. And while we were visiting, Lee, their boy, and Robin entertained us with a piano duet. Later, after leaving, we could not help but recall the recreations on television of Pa and Ma Ingalls in *Little House on the Prairie*.

Our first stop just had to be a visit to Plum Creek. This is the area Laura Ingalls Wilder wrote about in the Little House on the Prairie books. Also, Walnut Grove, Minnesota, was used for the setting of the popular television series.

What a pure delight for Robin and the rest of us to visit the banks of Plum Creek! There we viewed the hollow where Pa had built that first dugout. We enjoyed the natural beauty of this area on a beautiful spring day. Robin's familiarity with Laura's writings, together with her creative imagination, allowed her to put herself back in time. We could imagine her there with Laura and Mary, Jack close behind, running along Plum Creek.

After visiting the museum in Walnut Grove, we headed for De Smet, South Dakota. We wanted to see the Surveyors House where they lived during *The Long Winter*. The local people have also reconstructed an old schoolhouse typical of those early days. What a dramatic contrast with modern-day learning institutions!

We visited the Ingalls house in town. We had a relaxed time viewing the memorabilia they had collected. Our family appreciated the efforts these people have made to preserve a small part of their historical heritage.

It was difficult to get back on the road. We stopped at the cemetery to take pictures before reluctantly moving on. As we continued our journey, Robin and Ryan began rereading one of the Little House books to Rodger. Putting the people from the stories in the actual setting we had just visited brought the writings to life. We were too early in the season for the annual pageant but consoled ourselves with plans to return someday. On the next visit, we would also go to the site in Missouri where the family had finally settled.

Yankton, South Dakota, holds special significance for the Petrik family. My grandfather, Rudolf, and his brothers immigrated to this area from Bohemia in 1879. We had not planned to go that far south on this trip, but we were having so much fun traveling we decided to make a slight detour. Also, we could add a few more states for the kids to say where they had been. We briefly crossed over into Iowa and then down to Yankton and across the Missouri River into Nebraska.

The next few days would be one tourist stop after another. We pulled off the Interstate for our free glass of icy water at the world-famous Wall Drug Store. Next, we visited the Mount Rushmore area. This part of South Dakota had changed dramatically since my previous visit. The kids enjoyed viewing the presidents and listening to the story about this impressive accomplishment. Then we went spelunking, exploring one of many caverns. It soon became apparent it would be impossible to take in all the exciting attractions.

We needed to keep on schedule, so we headed for Yellowstone National Park. Being so early in the tourist season, we were surprised at the number of visitors already in the park. We did manage to get a cabin on Yellowstone Lake for one night. All of us enjoyed the awesome beauty of this naturally scenic place. There was still snow on the ground, and many of the wild animals were around the hot lakes. The boys enjoyed watching the buffalo, elk, moose, and deer close up. At one location, I talked Ryan into moving around behind a moose so I could get a better picture. Unfortunately, the animal was not in a cooperative mood. Poor Ryan was never in real jeopardy; however, he did make some fancy maneuvers in retreat.

We drove straight home from Yellowstone Park. As we traveled the many miles of highway, we had time to talk. We talked about the wonder and beauty of God's creation and the greatness of this nation of ours.

As a people, we, Americans, are truly blessed. The last two hundred miles or so, we were traveling late into the night. The excitement of the trip, as well as the anticipation of getting home, kept the kids from sleeping. We took the opportunity to give thanks to God for a safe journey and the enjoyment of the wonderful sights. Also, we thanked Him for the faith He gives us to believe and trust.

> For since the creation of the world God's invisible qualities—his eternal power and divine nature— have been clearly seen, being understood from what has been made, so that men are without excuse.
>
> Romans 1:20

Robin wanted to talk. She had some areas of real concern. She expressed a genuine fear of being brutalized by a bad person. Sometimes at night, while trying to go to sleep, she became frightened. Along with this was the fear she would not be ready to die and meet the Lord. We spent the next hour or so reviewing the assurance we have for Scripture.

Our faith, which is a gift from God, makes us acceptable to Him. This gives us the knowledge and peace that our sins are forgiven. As we act on this faith, we can overcome fear. We also know because God gave us His Spirit, a witness to live within our hearts. He will take care of our needs and provide for us just as surely as He has throughout that exhausting trip. And perchance, if our lives are shortened—by early death or a violent act—it will only be as God wills. By having this right relationship, we can have total assurance of our salvation. The powers of evil bring these doubts to our minds. We can get rid of them through faith, claiming His promises from Scripture.

We must realize we have Christ's new nature within us. The old sinful nature, still there, tries to put down this new relationship. Therefore, from time to time, we experience doubts and concerns. Because of this, we realize the importance of spending time studying God's Word and praying so that our faith is well-grounded. We become stronger as we uncover His provisions for humanity, but more personally, as we understand His perfect plan for our lives.

It was great to be home. The last few days of school went by very quickly, and vacation time started. Robin was doing babysitting; however, her goal for summer was to help at the pool. She loved to work with small children in addition to enjoying the water. When it came time for the pool to open, she was the first in line to see about a summer job. While she was only thirteen, not old enough to be an instructor, they could use her as an aide. Her assignment was to help with the beginners. She was ready!

She could hardly wait for September. Seventh graders were not allowed to hold major student body positions. She had been a class representative; however, to her, that was not good enough. Now, as an eighth grader, she had her heart set on running for Associated Student Body president.

Another volunteer position she just could not wait to take on was being a candy striper at one of the big hospitals in Spokane. But that would have to wait until she was fourteen. She was impatient with the idea one year could make such a difference.

Mapping the campaign strategy consumed much of the summer. She and her friends spent time gathering ideas. They reviewed last year's election and mapped out their plans. Robin almost became obsessed with the idea of winning. No matter how much we cautioned her about the real possibility of losing, she assured us she could handle the rejection. If she did not get enough votes, she promised not to be unduly upset.

She was ready when the school opened. It did not take long to get settled in with the new schedule of classes. The year before, she had completed all the junior-high math through algebra 2. The high school was offering a computer-science class, and four of them were picked to take it. Three days each week, they attended classes at the high school. It was a tight schedule: they had to get ten blocks back to junior high in time for the second period. Somehow, they managed. She loved all her studies.

It was time to start campaigning. She decided to run for president using one pet peeve and one exciting new idea. Her pet peeve was to get a needed sign. The sign out front of the junior high advertised the Deer Park High School. It had been three years since the high school had moved into its new facility. However, the sign had not been changed. Her exciting new idea was to start an exchange program with other junior highs. This could help develop a better understanding and relations among kids from different areas. Mr. Cain, the principal, had helped come up with the concept. Both were ambitious projects. Kay and I wondered about being able to make good on these kinds of campaign promises.

The busy summer had gotten away from us without any family-vacation time. We had wanted to go to Canada to the hot springs before school started. The press of other work and activities had precluded it. We felt the need to get away and relax and rescheduled our weekend trip for late September. As it happened, we were planning to leave at noon on the Friday of the big election.

As parents, we often overlook the abilities of our young people. I am afraid we were not as confident of Robin winning this important election as she was. We decided to keep our plans intact. If she did not get elected, she would have a little break away from the phone. We could help her reconcile her loss before returning to school Monday.

Instantly, we knew the results! When we arrived to pick them up, she almost floated toward the car on cloud nine. On the first ballot, she tied with another young man. However, she won the runoff by a landslide. She did not say it, but we knew what she was thinking: "O ye of little faith." Heading for Canada, and now our victory weekend, we gave thanks for this accomplishment. Also, we asked God to give Robin wisdom and understanding to do her absolute best at this important job.

She was following through on her campaign promises. By the time Christmas vacation started, all the details had been worked out. After taking office, she had appointed the necessary committees. The details of the new sign had to be worked out with the district superintendent. After several meetings, they got approval on the design and necessary funding. Working with sign contractors, they were finally able to settle on one that met everyone's criteria. The exchange-program committee completed a required feasibility report with its recommendations. This also had been approved. Plans were underway for selecting students to participate in and to contact other junior high schools.

Kay and I felt each family member was keeping things in perspective. Kay and Robin had a close relationship. They were able to share everything openly and with loving concern. Family communications seemed to be at an all-time high.

Ryan was adapting to the changes going on in junior high. Even to his role of little brother to the president (taller than sis by now). After a good football season, he was busy practicing basketball in the early mornings before school. Boys' basketball would start after they returned from Christmas vacation. Several of them were getting a head start on the season with these extra practices.

Rodger had second grade under control. He was very rapidly developing his reading and math skills. His least exciting subject was French. His only major complaint was he could not understand why the elementary school did not have a football and basketball team. He consoled himself by looking forward to spring soccer.

Robin really enjoyed this junior-high year. The role of the president was everything she had hoped. She continued doing exceptionally well with her schoolwork and music. One of her teachers commented on this, indicating she was becoming a real perfectionist. Not in a bad sense, but realistically pushing herself to the maximum while retaining enough flexibility not to become frustrated.

She was a typical teenager—not everything was perfect: for one thing, she felt she did not have any friends. And something else bothered her to no end. The youth group and Sunday school class were not getting into enough in-depth Bible study to suit her. As far as friends go, we felt this was probably normal with young people of her age. They do tend to be a "little fickle." She thought she might be slightly guilty in this area herself and determined to work on it.

The youth group was a different matter. Robin talked with Jack Grimm, the youth pastor. This still did not seem satisfactory, so out came the pen and paper to write down her thoughts. After several days, she decided to give it to him.

She approached her Sunday school teacher a little differently. As a true politician, somehow, she convinced him to let her have the opportunity to teach one lesson. In this way, she could demonstrate how she felt by making the material a little more thought-provoking. He agreed, which really pleased her.

There is no question about this being a difficult stage in growing up. These problems notwithstanding, Robin was finding answers. Through personal Bible study, discussions, and family devotions, she was readily developing spiritual convictions and faith. This, along with her background from Sunday school and the Awana program, was a significant help to her in working through the problematic area.

For you to better understand things: she kept a special notebook, "Time Out" (see the Appendix section), in which to record her findings. Occasionally, she shared a page with friends experiencing a similar type of question. She asked Kay and me not to read it as she felt it might embarrass her.

She was looking forward to her fourteenth birthday. She had already made up her mind it was not going to be the most exciting event but necessary to get to fifteen. It would be fun getting her driving permit. Fourteen was just kind of an event sandwiched in between.

That year, Grandma and Grandpa Nelson intended to spend two weeks with us. Usually, they came for a short visit near Christmas. It had always been a very rushed three or four days. Not that year: they wanted to spend extra time enjoying the grandkids. Besides, Robin and Grandma enjoyed shopping. What better opportunity to do this than to take in the after-Christmas sales and specials?

Robin went for her annual checkup early. Kay thought it would be a good idea to complete it earlier, as we would be having company in January. The clinic in Seattle had transferred Robin's records to Spokane, which saved us from having to make a special trip across the mountains during winter. The checkup was completed, as scheduled, on December 22. The blood tests and X-rays were all excellent. No problems whatsoever, kidney or anything else. The doctor's parting comment was, "You can expect to live to be an old lady."

The same week also included the annual Christmas programs. Rodger's school was first. Theirs had a Scandinavian touch. Robin and Ryan's concert was a pleasant mixture of both Christmas and contemporary music. President Robin did the announcing and played piano and synthesizer. Ryan was one of the drummers. Similarly, each of them had a part in the presentation at church. Robin's was a solo part in an upbeat contemporary Christian song. She literally danced her way into the hearts of those attending. Her ability to add sparkle as needed to an occasion and her personal confidence when entertaining really showed forth her love of people and willingness to share the talents God had given her.

8

Angel's Call

Our Christmas was especially nice. It fell on Sunday, which required changes in our usual routine. Normally, we would open presents on Christmas morning. Christmas Eve was Robin's special birthday time. She oversaw the delicate and complicated family negotiations to make the necessary rearrangements to everyone's satisfaction.

We would celebrate her birthday on the twenty-third, the day the Nelsons arrived. This left Christmas morning free to attend services, a very refreshing and meaningful way to remember Jesus's birth. Part of the worship service was devoted to observing the Lord's Supper.

This early church tradition, Communion, or, as some refer to it, the Lord's Supper, has been practiced by Christians since the night of Judas's betrayal.

> While they were eating, Jesus took the bread, gave thanks, and broke it and gave it to his disciples, saying, "Take and eat; this is my body." Then he took the cup, gave thanks, and offered it to them, saying, "Drink from it, all of you. This is my blood of the cov-

enant, which is poured out for many for the forgiveness of sins."

Matthew 26:26–28

For whenever you eat this bread and drink from this
cup, you proclaim the Lord's death until he comes.

1 Corinthians 11:26

The real joy in celebrating Christ's birth is found in the significance of His shed blood. This is the only way we can have
forgiveness for our sins.

On the twenty-sixth, Robin and her grandmother were in
downtown Spokane for the after-Christmas events. They even
talked Kay into fighting the crowds with them.

Our weather was turning very wintry with extreme cold
and blowing snow. Grandad was thankful they were not rushing home. We were having a wonderful old-fashioned holiday.
Even the leftovers tasted good. We tried to make the joyous season last as long as possible.

Early in the morning hours of December 30, Robin got sick.
It appeared to be some sort of flu bug with a high fever, vom-
iting, and diarrhea. None of our family had been seriously ill
for some time. We easily bounced back from the usual bouts
of winter flu and colds by taking aspirin or Tylenol, extra fluids, and rest. Mom gave Robin a couple of Tylenol. The fever
seemed to be coming down, and Robin went back to bed.

About four o'clock, she got worse. The fever was back, and it
was a little difficult for her to breathe. She joked with her mom
about rolling her in the snow to cool off. This commotion woke

me up. I went to see what was going on. It did not seem serious, especially since she had just gotten a clean bill of health from her checkup. However, with the continuing high fever, we decided to take her to the local hospital. On the way, Robin commented, "Mom, I don't want to die."

At the emergency room, the nurse called Dr. Stime, our family doctor. While we were waiting for him, the nurses went ahead with preliminary blood tests. One of them worked at trying to get the fever down. When the doctor arrived, he ordered a chest X-ray and then reviewed the blood tests. He concluded she had some sort of bacteria or virus. The chest X-ray did not indicate any alarming amount of congestion. Next, he went with me through the available list of antibiotics to determine which one to use. He asked about allergic reactions to specific drugs, to which she had none, and then ordered the medicine.

Robin had a slight seizure and became somewhat disoriented. The doctor decided to have the nurse administer the antibiotic intravenously so it could rapidly start fighting off the bug. It was about quarter to five when he left, saying he would be back in a couple of hours. Robin should have some relief by that time.

Within a very few minutes, her condition deteriorated. Kay and I were chitchatting with her when the disorientation returned. She started talking about the presents she had gotten the boys for Christmas and was wondering if they had opened them yet. Then she asked, "Where are you?" Suddenly, we realized her eyesight had failed. In just the next few seconds, she had a cardiopulmonary failure.

Since this was a small community hospital, there were only two nurses on duty. Kay ran down the hall to telephone our doctor while one of the nurses and I administered CPR. The other nurse went to get the emergency equipment ready. Kay also called our pastor and asked him to pray with us about her condition.

We worked feverishly trying to keep oxygen in her lungs; however, they kept filling with fluids. Unbelievably, her body systems just continued to shut down.

Another doctor arrived. He administered adrenalin and started defibrillation. They called the "Life Bird," a critical emergency helicopter team from Spokane. Our doctor returned. The weather was so bad that the helicopter could not fly, so they would drive in an emergency vehicle arriving in about thirty minutes.

Together, we had done everything humanly and medically possible.

God's angels simply came down and carried Robin away to be with Him.

The clock on the wall read 6:30 a.m.

***

Little Robin flew away;
Part of her will always stay,
Tucked in our hearts, and when we pray,
We'll remember Robin.

The spiritual insights Robin had
Were tender and sweet, never sad.
She sought the good, rejected the bad.
We're proud of Robin.

Loving knowledge of God's Word,
With the understanding of what she heard,
She gave testimony of sacred things,
And now she's safely
Under His wings!

In loving tribute to Robin Petrik,
by S. Luther Essick,
poet friend

9

Her Friends

"I felt, in a way, like she was very close, and yet, I didn't even talk to her much."

—Crystal (seventh-grade girl)

"She was a very special friend of mine. She had a lot going for her; she was a great Christian. Now she's with the Lord."

—Nichole, Chicago (eighth-grade girl)

"I grew to have tremendous admiration and respect for her. Robin's maturity and understanding extended beyond her years. We miss Robin every day, but our memories are filled with fondness and joy."

—a science teacher

"I've been a Christian since I was a little girl but just haven't been acting like it. I haven't been acting it or living it because I wouldn't or didn't have the time. Hearing how much she was in the Word has helped me a lot. I started a Bible study."

—Beckey (high school girl)

"I think I was close to Robin, but she was also friends with everyone else. Robin was one of a kind, and we had a special relationship. Words can't explain how I felt about Robin."

—Kristin (eighth-grade girl)

"I remember Robin as a person who gave 100 percent of herself in everything she did."

—Trish (swimming instructor)

"Robin was not only the most qualified to die but also the most qualified to live."

—Jack (youth pastor)

"Memories are something no one can ever take. We all loved her and always will."

—unsigned (classmate)

"Robin has been so very special [...] have given so sacrificially of yourself."

—Sharon (friend)

"Robin was a leader, never afraid to do what she thought was right."

—unsigned (classmate)

"Special memories that no one can ever take away."

—Nicole (eighth-grade girl)

"Very often called 'Bobin,' she was loved and wanted and will be missed."

—unsigned (classmate)

"She was everyone's pal; she was an outgoing gal; we all loved her so, but who would think it would be her? The president, the one everyone looked up to [...] The life she lived is the one that everyone wants to have. Her relationship with friends [...] We'll miss her smile."

—unsigned (classmate)

"Think of Robin: laugh, don't cry; I know she'd want it that way. A friend of a friend, a friend to the end. I think you are here taking our tears away!"

—unsigned (classmate)

"Each morning when I walked into school, Robin would always come up to me and say, "Hi, Gena, how's it going?" I really miss her very much."

—Regina (seventh-grade girl)

"She listened; she cared; she helped, and she gave hope. Robin believed the best things should never be kept, they must be given away—a smile, a hug, a kiss. She gave the best she had, and we are better because of it."

—Mr. Cain (principal)

Postscript

Adventure Complete

"Sweet Robin"
I wish there were words to say
To help in taking your hurt away.
I know that Robin is in His hand,
But it's so hard to understand.

So many things only last a while—
A rainbow, rose, a lovely smile.
I only know it's God's plan
To share our grief and understand.

by S. Luther Essick

In the days following Robin's "homecoming," we tried to cope. It was difficult to focus on reality. It was so sudden and unexpected we were in a state of shock. An autopsy was ordered. We needed to make final arrangements.

As we were talking about making the service a fitting memorial, Kay recalled Robin's notebook. As we read through it, our hearts could only give praise to God for loaning us this very special daughter. Each page revealed her strong commitment to the Lord. Her special understanding of His will and His desire to help in every situation gave us special comfort and strength.

Friends began dropping in and calling to offer their condolences. Her friends were in such a state of disbelief they phoned asking for Robin and, upon having confirmation of her death, would hang up without giving their names.

Robin's adventure was complete. Her life was so perfectly in order she had not left anything undone. Everything was in readiness in the event God should call for her, not only in her spiritual life but in every area. She had no relationships that needed mending, no forgiveness to ask of anyone; her room was picked up and neat; her homework completed, and Kay's birthday present purchased and wrapped (her mom's birthday was on January 3).

It is our earnest desire, in understanding God's will and plan, to share our lives and Robin's to bring honor and glory to our heavenly Father. God was at work from the very beginning; we never received billing from Children's Orthopedic Hospital, University Hospital, nor any of the doctors—they classified it as exploratory research. Robin was the first child to be successful on chronic peritoneal dialysis and the youngest child ever successfully transplanted, pioneering a much brighter future for other children.

"So that, just as sin reigned in death, so also, grace might reign through righteousness to bring eternal life through Jesus our Lord" (Romans 5:21).

Our prayer is that Robin's dedication and service to God will be an inspiration and help to you on your adventure through life, whether you are just beginning, nearing completion, or somewhere in between. If you do not know our God, Jesus Christ, our risen Lord and Savior, you need to repent from your sins and let Him into your heart and life. It is the only way to find peace and assurance for heaven.

"Jesus answered, 'I am the way and the truth and the life. No one comes to the Father except through me'" (John 14:6).

God's perfect will revealed to us through His Word is for everyone and everything to bring honor and glory to Him. Each of us is a part of His creation. Robin has done this. Through these writings, her life will continue honoring God. Robin wrote:

"Thanks, Lord, for loving me so much and not even expecting anything in return—I will serve You because I want to! Amen."

Notes

1 Jim Saville, originally written by Edgar Albert Guest, "A Child Of Mine," as quoted in All Poetry, accessed October 18, 2021, https://allpoetry.com/A-Child-Of-Mine.

2 Corrie ten Boom, "Life is but a Weaving" (The Tapestry Poem), as quoted in The Poetry Place, accessed October 18, 2021, https://thepoetryplace.wordpress.com/2018/02/21/ life-is-but-a-weaving-the-tapestry-poem-by-corrie-ten-boom.

Appendix

Robin's Notebook

"Time Out"

Robin's Notebook

This book contains help for specific problems and some
overviews of some of the books of the Bible.

Good Works cannot save you
and are not required.

Romans 4:5
Romans 6:23
Acts 16:31
Titus 2:11
Ephesians 2:8-9

God saved us because he
had mercy on us + he loved
us so much. We don't have
to do one extra thing to be
saved but we should want to
tell others + be good - but again
we don't need to, to be saved.
We will, though be asked, +
honored + held accountable for
any good deeds we've done.

Thanks Lord for loving me
so much + not even expecting
anything in return - I will
serve you because I want to! Amen

"However, to the man who does not work but trusts God who justifies the wicked, his faith is credited as righteousness."

Romans 4:5

"For the wages of sin is death, but the gift of God is eternal life in Christ Jesus our Lord."

Romans 6:23

"They replied, 'Believe in the Lord Jesus, and you will be saved—you and your household.'"

Acts 16:31

"For the grace of God that brings salvation has appeared to all men."

Titus 2:11

"For it is by grace you have been saved, through faith—and this not from yourselves, it is the gift of God—not by works, so no one will boast."

Ephesians 2:8–9

Having faith in hard times

James 5:13
James 1:2
1 Peter 5:7
Romans 8:28
Luke 12:22 & Matthew 6:25
Phillipians 4:6

God can't try our faith in good times but he can see it really shine through, or not shine at all in bad times. He gives us bad times, physically financially, & emotionally for 2 reasons. 1. To see how much faith we really have. 2. so we can appreciate the good times even more. We should pray that he will help us through it & then in our hearts we can have God's peace.

Philippians 4:7

And remember to tell God all out it (but don't blame him) Il feel better - ask for peace.

"Is any one of you in trouble? He should pray. Is anyone happy? Let him sing songs of praise."

James 5:13

"Consider it pure joy, my brothers, whenever you face trials of many kinds, because you know that the testing of your faith develops perseverance."

James 1:2

"Cast all your anxiety on him because he cares for you."

1 Peter 5:7

"And we know that in all things God works for the food of those who love him, who have been called according to his purpose."

Romans 8:28

"Then Jesus said to his disciples: 'Therefore I tell you, do not worry about your life, what you will eat; or about your body, what you will wear.'"

Luke 12:22

"Therefore I tell you, do not worry about your life, what you will eat or drink; or about your body, what you will wear. Is not life more important than food, and the body more important than clothes?"

Matthew 6:25

"Do not be anxious about anything, but in everything, by prayer and petition, with thanksgiving, present your requests to God."

Philippians 4:6

"And the peace of God, which transcends all understanding, will guard your hearts and your minds in Christ Jesus."

Philippians 4:7

Gods love for us.

John 3:16   1 am. 3:22

1 John 4:10   1 John 4:16

Romans 5:8   Psalm 36:7

Ephesians 2:4   GO TO - POEMS & SAYINGS

1 Peter 5:7   NO. 1

If I could, I would put every verse in the bible on this page, because practically every verse is there because he loves us so much. He knew about you when he sent his son & he has a special life for you because of his love. He let his very own son die, just for me & I still don't deserve it. He will always love us. It's up to you to turn away, but he never will. No sin is too great to be forgiven, + when the wall (made by sin) is broken down (or forgiven) God can come in to you and live forever with peace.
Thank him for his love for you.

"For God so loved the world that he gave his one and only Son, that whoever believes in him shall not perish by have eternal life."

John 3:16

"This is love: not that we loved God, but that he loved us and sent his Son as an atoning sacrifice for our sins."

1 John 4:10

"But God demonstrates his own love for us in this: While we were still sinners, Christ died for us."

Romans 5:8

"But because of his great love for us, God, who is rich in mercy, made us alive with Christ even when we were dead in transgressions—it is by grace you have been saved."

Ephesians 2:4–5

"Cast all your anxiety on him because he cares for you."

1 Peter 5:7

"Because of the LORD's great love we are not consumed, for his compassions never fail."

Lamentations 3:22

"And so we know and rely on the love God has for us. God is love. Whoever lives in love lives in God and God in him."

1 John 4:16

"How priceless is your unfailing love! Both high and low among men find refuge in the shadow of your wings."

Psalm 36:7

When your scared at
   Psalm 145:20 night
   Psalm 4:8
   Psalm 23:4
   1 John 4:18
When you get scared
try this: pray to God,
   then sing to him, read
the bible + think about
something else. Ast God for
peace + try to sleep. We
have to have some ~~faith~~ faith -
like it says in the
bible - "what will one minute
of worrying add to your
life?"
Its not easy to do - but
it will pass -
Be sure to have faith in
him.

Dear Lord -
I need you right now - come to me,
fill me, give me more faith - give
me peace, I give you my life - I love
you - AMEN

"The LORD watches over all who love him, but all the wicked he will destroy."

Psalm 145:20

"I will lie down and sleep in peace, for you alone, O Lord, make me dwell in safety."

Psalm 4:8

"Even though I walk through the valley of the shadow of death, I will fear no evil, for you are with me: your rod and staff, they comfort me."

Psalm 23:4, ESV

"There is no fear in love, but perfect love drives out fear, because fear has to do with punishment. The man who fears is not made perfect in love."

1 John 4:18

You cannot lose your
Salvation.

John 5:24
Acts 16:31
John 3:16
John 3:15

There is no way that
God is going to let go of
you once you have honestly
with your whole heart-
have him living in you,
when you do this he forgives
you for your sins that are
gonna happen tomorrow -
So you can't lose it!
You have to have faith -
after all that is what
salvation is based on isn't it?
Stick with god & he'll stick
with you -
Tell it
to God - & he can help
you feel it - but you need
faith!

"I tell you the truth, whoever hears my word and believes him who sent me has eternal life and will not be condemned; he has crossed over from death to life."

John 5:24

"They replied, 'Believe in the Lord Jesus, and you will be saved—you and your household.'"

Acts 16:31

"For God so loved the world that he gave his one and only Son, that whoever believes in him shall not perish but have eternal life."

John 3:16

"[...] that everyone who believes in him may have eternal life."

John 3:15)

Love for people

Ephesians 4:32
1 John 4:7-8
1 Corinthians 4-6
1 Corinthians 13:13
1 John 4:19

Now, we know

1. who to love — Everyone.
2. Why to love — Because he first loved us
3. when to love — all the time.
4. and how to love 1 Corin. 13:4-6

God is patient, kind, protecting, trusting, hoping, + preserving. His love never envies, He doesn't boast, He's love isn't proud, or rude, or self seeking, or easily angered, it doesn't delight in evil + rejoices with the truth - If he loves us like that shouldn't that be how we love others? It is hard to love others but just pray for His love for them - God loves - so we must love!

"Be kind and compassionate to one another, forgiving each other, just as in Christ God forgave you."

Ephesians 4:32

"Dear friends, let us love one another, for love comes from God. Everyone who loves has been born of God and knows God. Whoever does not love does not know God, because God is love."

1 John 4:7–8

"Love is patient, love is kind. It does not envy, it does not boast, it is not proud. It is not rude, it is not self-seeking, it is not easily angered, it keeps no record of wrongs. Love does not delight in evil but rejoices with the truth."

1 Corinthians 13:4–6

"And these three remain: faith, hope and love, but the greatest of these is love."

1 Corinthians 13:13

"We love because he first loved us."

1 John 4:19

When will He come?

1 Thesselonians 5:2
Revelation 22:7
Matthew 24
Mark 13

Don't be scared when people say - "I know He's coming Today." Because NOBODY KNOWS WHEN HE'S COMING - because if they did they would wait till the last minute and Jesus doesn't want that you should ALWAYS be ready - and don't be scared - and don't want to stay - for "where your treasure is there your heart may be also"

God won't come when everyones expecting him but be ready - he's coming soon!

Also, don't let earthquakes, floods, eruptions, irregular weather patterns + an unusual amount of sin get you down - these are birth pains of what is yet to come - ASK God to help you - He'll give you

"For you know very well that the day of the Lord will come like a thief in the night."

1 Thessalonians 5:2

"Behold, I am coming soon! Blessed is he who keeps the words of the prophecy in this book."

Revelations 22:7

"No one knows about that day or hour, not even the angels in heaven, nor the Son, but only the Father. As it was in the days of Noah, so it will be at the coming of the Son of Man. For in the days before the flood, people were eating and drinking, marrying, and giving in marriage, up to the day Noah entered the ark; and they knew nothing about what would happen until the flood came and took them all away. That is how it will be at the coming of the Son of Man. Two men will be in the field; one will be taken and the other left. Two women will be grinding with a hand mill; one will be taken and the other left.
"Therefore, keep watch, because you do not know on what day your Lord will come. But understand this: if the owner of the house had known at what time of night the thief was coming, he would have kept watch and would not have let his house be broken into. So, you also must be ready, because the Son of Man will come at an hour when you do not expect him"

Matthew 24:36–44

Mark, chapter thirteen is a similar account.

When you don't like
yourself (your body)

Psalm 63:3
1 Cor. 15:10
Psalm 139:13-16
Eccles. 3:11

I'm too fat, my hair is so
ugly, I have a pimple on the end
of my nose so BIG I can't see
over it - How come I can't be
more like the prettiest girl
in school?
God made you special.
When you act like the "above
you are criticizing his
work. You should thank him
for everything you like about
you and as for the things you
don't like - try to change your
hairstyle to cheer you up - thank
him for the parts you don't
like th think how lucky you
are because some people don't
even have some of them -

"Because your love is better than life, my lips will glorify you."

Psalm 63:3

"But by the grace of God I am what I am, and his grace to me was not without effect. No, I worked harder than all of them—yet not I, but the grace of God that was with me."

1 Corinthians 15:10

"For you created my inmost being; you knit me together in by mothers' womb. I praise you because I am fearfully and wonderfully made; your works are wonderful; I know that full well. My frame was not hidden from you when I was made in the secret place. When I was woven together in the depths of the earth, your eyes saw my unformed body. All the days ordained for me were written in your book before any of them came to be."

Psalm 139:13–16

"He has made everything beautiful in its time. He has also set eternity in the hearts of men; yet they cannot fathom what God has done from the beginning to end."

Ecclesiastes 3:11

James OLD - (NEW) TESTAMENT

James is writing a
letter to the 12 tribes of.
scattered among the nations
James has a lot to help
you be a better person
he talks about having
faith in the bad times, prayer,
listening & doing, temptation,
favoritism, faith & deeds,
taming the tongue, submit-
ting yourself to God, &
swearing.
Its 5 chapters long - I
think you should read it.

Key Verses:
    James 5:13
     "   "   4:7
     "   "   1:2

"Is anyone of you in trouble? He should pray. Is anyone happy? Let him sing songs of praise."

James 5:13

"Submit yourselves, then, to God. Resist the devil, and he will flee from you."

James 4:7

"Consider it pure joy, my brothers, whenever you face trials of many kinds."

James 1:2

Jonah & the fish

Lets take a quiz -
1. How long was Jonah
in the fish? Jonah 1:17

2. what was the first
thing he did? Jonah 2:1

3. How did he get there?
   Jonah 1

Have you ever thought about
what it was like in there?
The smell would be nauseating
you would be tossed & turned
It would be hot & stuffy
Some people even believe the
stomach acids may have
bleached his skin, hair &
then to be thrown up & out
of it. you would have had NO
Food, or water, either.

Jonah was running

"But the LORD provided a great fish to swallow Jonah, and Jonah was inside the fish three days and three nights."

Jonah 1:17

"From inside the fish Jonah prayed to the LORD his God."

Jonah 2:1

"Then they took Jonah and threw him overboard, and the raging sea grew calm."

Jonah 1:15

Death & Jonah Cont.
from God. Death could
happen at any time. If
we dont have God on our
side we could spend eternity
in Hell. If death really
"FREAKS you OUT" think
of it this way: "Death is
the beginning of your
eternal life.
Its your choice where
to spend it

James 4:14

"Why, you do not even know what will happen tomorrow. What is your life? You are a mist that appears for a little while and then vanishes."

James 4:14

How to pray

Matthew 6:9
John 17

When you are confused about the right way to pray, you really shouldn't be: There are some people who believe you should pray like Jesus did: Be sincere in your prayers, & they'll come out right. Here are some pointers:

1. You should probably ask forgiveness <u>first</u> to have a clear conscious

2. Thank him for everything

3. Ask your needs & explain all your problems in detail.
    James 5:13-18

"This is how you should pray: 'Our Father in heaven, hallowed be your name, your kingdom come, your will be done, on earth as it is in heaven. Give us today our daily bread. Forgive us our debts, as we also have forgiven our debtors. And lead us not into temptation but deliver us from the evil one'."

Matthew 6:9–13

In John 17, Jesus prays.

"And the prayer offered in faith will make the sick person well; the Lord will raise him up. If he has sinned, he will be forgiven. Therefore, confess your sins to each other and pray for each other so that you may be healed. The prayer of a righteous man is powerful and effective. Elijah was a man just like us. He prayed earnestly that it would not rain, and it did not rain of the land for three and a half years. Again, he prayed, and the heavens gave rain, and the earth produced its crops."

James 5:15–18

What is God Like?

God is like:

God is like Coke: He's the real thing
God is like General Electric: He lights your path
God is like Bayer Aspirin: He works wonders
God is like Tide: He gets the stain out
God is like Hair Spray: He holds through it all
God is like Dial Soap: Aren't you glad you know him?
God is like Sears: He has everything
God is like Alka Seltzer: Try him, you'll like him
God is like scotch tape: you can't see him but you know he's there.
God is like Hallmark Cards:

He cares enough to send the very best

Psalm 145:8
Psalm 145:9

"The LORD is gracious and compassionate, slow to anger and rich in love. The LORD is good to all; he has compassion on all he has made."

Psalm 145:8–9

That Tongue of Yours

Ephesians 4:29-32

We hurt people all the time (and its a deep hurt) with our words. If there's a twinge of anger, or another bit of feeling, they can detect it.

I'm not talking of swearing
JAMES 5:12
You can't take away what you've said, and make the other person forget it, but you **can** stop it before it gets to the "tip of your tongue"

Ask yourself this: When a person goes away from talking with me, how do they feel? Try to make that answer "wonderful." One more thing- Don't gossip.

"Do not let any unwholesome talk come out of your mouths, but only what is helpful for building others up according to their needs, that it may benefit those who listen. And do not grieve the Holy Spirit of God, with whom you were sealed for the day of redemption. Get rid of all bitterness, rage, and anger, brawling and slander, along with every form of malice. Be kind and compassionate to one another, forgiving each other, just as in Christ God forgave you."

Ephesians 4:29–32

"Above all, my brothers, do not swear—not by heaven or by earth or by anything else. Let your 'Yes' be yes, and your 'No' no, or you will be condemned."

James 5:12

Take up the Armor of God

Ephesians 6:10-18

I want to be strong in the Lord!
YOU DO TO!
This can help you stand up
against the devils temptings
Put these on:
The <u>Belt</u> of truth

<u>Breastplate</u> of righteousness

<u>feet</u> fitted with readiness

<u>Shield</u> of faith

<u>helmet</u> of salvation and

the <u>sword</u> of the spirit -

I think this would be great
to memorize so when your
scared or lonely you can have
Strength! — AMEN!

"Finally, be strong in the Lord and in his mighty power. Put on the full armor of God so that you can take your stand against the devil's schemes. For our struggle is not against flesh and blood, but against the rulers, against the authorities, against the powers of this dark world and against the spiritual forces of evil in the heavenly realms. Therefore, put on the full armor of God, so that when the day of evil comes, you may be able to stand your ground, and after you have done everything, to stand. Stand firm then, with the belt of truth buckled around your waist, with the breastplate of righteousness in place, and with your feet fitted with the readiness that comes from the gospel of peace. In addition to all this, take up the shield of faith, with which you can extinguish all the flaming arrows of the evil one. Take the helmet of salvation and the sword of the Spirit, which is the Word of God. And pray in the Spirit on all occasions with all kinds of prayers and requests. With this in mind, be alert and always keep on praying for all the saints."

Ephesians 6:10–18

Contract

DECLARATION

We, Dad and Mom, feel it is necessary not to create lists of rules, regulations, and privileges but to live in a righteous and prudent manner.

We also know that the law is made not for good men but for the lawbreakers and rebels, the ungodly and sinful, the unholy and irreligious; for those who kill their fathers or mothers, for murderers, for adulterers and perverts, for slave traders and liars and perjures—and for whatever else is contrary to the sound doctrine that conforms to the glorious gospel of the blessed God, which he entrusted to me.

1 Timothy 1:9–11

We resolve that for twelve years, we have endeavored to bring you up in the nurture and admonition of our Lord, having tried to instill in you values that will serve you for the rest of your life, tried by example, not always successfully, to *put God first and show kindness, fairness, and concern not only for you and our family but to those around us.*

We resolve that together, we can, during the next seven years, continue our relationship of love, trust, and responsibility to each other. "Children, obey your parents in the Lord, for this is right. 'Honor your father and mother'—which is the first commandment with a promise—'so that it may go well with you and that you may enjoy long life on the earth'" (Ephesians 6:1–3). We further resolve that having freedom from rules and regulations brings with it responsibility, the responsibility of making correct choices. With the Lord's guidance, we have helped you make those choices during the past twelve years. Now you will be making increased choices on your own. Further, we do believe this also gives us a parental right to change our position should it become evident that the resolution of this agreement is being violated while you are in the process of becoming an adult.

We resolve that during the next seven years, as you grow into adulthood, we are not always going to be there at your side. The difficulty of being a teenager is in developing your own rules and regulations. Certainly, we are not always going to agree on which are correct or incorrect; however, we pledge to try to be understanding and supportive of you and to give you guidance. Being open and honest with each other will strengthen our relationship, and we are confident, with the Lord's help, each of us will survive the teenage years, and you will grow into a mature loving Christian adult.

We resolve: "Do your best to present yourself to God as one approved, a workman who does not need to be ashamed and who correctly manages the word of truth" (2 Timothy 2:15). We resolve that privileges are rewards for approved conduct and workmanship.

We resolve that we love you very much and pray that you will follow our Lord's command, "And thou shalt love the Lord thy God with all thy heart, and with all thy soul, and all thy mind, and with all thy strength [...] Thou shalt love thy neighbor as thyself. There is none other commandment greater than these" (Mark 12:30–31, KJV). Study and follow God's Word, for, in it, all the answers to this adventure called life are contained. God bless you.

With our love and prayers,
Dad and Mom

CPSIA information can be obtained
at www.ICGtesting.com
Printed in the USA
BVHW040218140322
631396BV00017B/331